Revelation Forever!

Roger A. Hubbard
Th.M., D.Min.

Revelation ... Forever!

First Edition 2008, Third Printing 2017

Westcliff Press, P.O. Box 1521, Amarillo TX 79105, 1-806-359-6362
www.webtheology.com. Printed in the United States of America

ISBN: 9780991358564
Library of Congress Catalog Card Number 2014935680

"Scripture taken from the *NEW AMERICAN STANDARD BIBLE®*, © Copyright 1960, 1962, 1963, 1968, 1971, 1972, 1973, 1975, 1977, 1995 by The Lockman Foundation. Used by permission." (www.Lockman.org)

Suggested Cataloging-in Data

Hubbard, Roger Alan
    Revelation ... Forever! / Roger Alan Hubbard
    p. 24cm
    Includes Biblical references, Illustrations
    1. Bible - Theology. Theology - Doctrinal. Bible - Research.
    Suggested Library of Congress Number: BS543: Suggested Dewey Number: 230.041

....

Cover

From a picture by Pat Marvenko Smith. Used by permission. Art used by permission, Pat Marvenko Smith, ©1992 (www.revelationillustrated.com/artist.asp)

Dedication

To the congregation of the Lake Tanglewood Community Church, Amarillo, Texas, without whose love and support this book would not have been published. .

About the Author

Dr. Roger A. Hubbard is a 1976 graduate of the Dallas Theological Seminary, and earned his Doctorate of Ministry from The Christian Bible College and Seminary. His pastoral ministry extends from 1976, and includes four churches; he has been the Pastor of the Lake Tanglewood Community Church in Amarillo, TX since 1999. Dr. Hubbard and his wife, Lorna, have three children and nine grandchildren.

Foreword

The title, *Revelation ... Forever!* comes from the theme of the book of the Revelation, "Jesus Christ will rightfully rule on the earth." When Jesus comes again, as the book prophetically shows, He will come in power and glory to take over planet earth, and will rule forever. Christians should be living their lives in anticipation of His return, because it could happen today!

Why do we need another book about the last book of the Bible? For several reasons:

(1) It is a fascinating study because most of the book is unfulfilled prophecy. We should strive to understand its meaning. *Revelation ... Forever* includes a detailed study of the Greek text, whose definitions shed light on a shadowy subject

(2) The Book of Revelation is an enigma. Overall it is written in a strict chronological order. However, after each of the chapters that reveal God's future judgments, God the Holy Spirit has written chapters that "flashback" to fill in details of the period of the Tribulation. Unless the reader is aware of these "flashbacks," the book seems to violate its own chronology and leaves the reader confused. These "flashbacks" are carefully identified in *Revelation ... Forever.* After each flashback, the book returns to its strict chronological order

(3) If biblical prophecy is "pre-written history," a fresh comparison of the Book of Revelation to current events will encourage the unbeliever to trust in Christ for the forgiveness of sins, because His return is imminent. Also, the book will encourage believers to live each day in obedience to His Word, for it says in Revelation 22:12, "My reward is with Me." Revelation 20:6 says that believers will rule and reign with Christ for 1,000 years; it is, therefore, reasonable to conclude that our present obedience to Him will directly determine our position in His government when He returns. Perhaps *Revelation ... Forever* will inspire the reader to take another look at their own daily walk with Jesus Christ.

Author's Note

Extra care has been taken to include the verses of the Book of Revelation within the text of *Revelation ... Forever!* This saves the reader the time and effort in looking back and forth from his or her Bible to the text. Furthermore, the Bible is its own commentary; as reference is made to relevant parallel passages from the Scriptures, they are included here to save time. It is hoped that this facilitates the study and confirms the interpretations made.

Revelation ... Forever!

Theme of the Book: Jesus Christ will rightfully rule on the earth.

Basis of the Outline: Revelation 1:19, the "things which you *have seen,* and the things which *are,* and the things which *shall take place* after these things."

Outline

I. **Past** - "write the things which you have seen." **p. 7**

A. John introduces the book and salutes the churches. **p. 7**
1. The Prologue. **p. 7**
2. Salutation to the Churches. **p. 11**
B. John describes what he has seen; the resurrected, glorified Son of God, Jesus Christ. **p. 21**

II. **Present** - "write the things which are." **p. 29**
A. The Letter to Ephesus. **p. 29**
B. The Letter to Smyrna. **p. 35**
C. The Letter to Pergamum. **p. 41**
D. The Letter to Thyatira. **p. 46**
E. The Letter to Sardis. **p. 51**
F. The Letter to Philadelphia. **p. 59**
G. The Letter to Laodicea. **p. 65**

III. **Future** - "write the things which shall take place." **p. 72**

A. Heavenly preparation for the Great Tribulation. **p. 72**

1. God is recognized and worshipped in heaven (Rev. 4:1-11). **p. 72**
2. The Book of God's redemption is given to Christ (Rev. 5:1-14). **p.80**
B. The Great Tribulation. **p. 88**
1. The first half of the Tribulation (Rev. 6 and 7). **p. 88**
a. The Seven Seal Judgments (Rev. 6:1-17). **p. 88**
b. The first "flashback:" God seals His witnesses (Rev. 7:1-17). **p. 95**
2. The second half of the Tribulation (Rev. 8-18). **p. 102**
a. The Seven Trumpet Judgments (Rev. 8:1-9, 21). **p. 102**
b. The second "flashback:" description of events during the first and second halves of the Tribulation (Rev. 10-14). **p. 115**

Illustrations

Revelation ... Forever

I. Past - "write the things which you have seen," Chapter 1.

A. John introduces the Book and salutes the churches (Revelation 1:1-8).

1. The Prologue - This is the Revelation of Jesus Christ.

> ▶ *The Revelation of Jesus Christ, which God gave Him to show to His bond-servants, the things which must soon take place; and He sent and communicated it by His angel to His bond-servant John [Revelation 1:1].*

Revelation is the Greek word *apokalupsis*,[1] which means an unveiling, a disclosure, a *revelation* (of that which was before concealed). It gives our English word *apocalypse*, meaning to uncover; it is used to refer to the Book of Revelation and is sometimes used to mean the judgments of the end of the world. *Of Jesus Christ* is probably a subjective genitive, meaning that Jesus Christ is the Subject, the doer of the action. *God* is God the Father, who is the One giving the Revelation to God the Son, who is giving it *to His bond-servant John*. In the Holy Trinity, God the Father plans, God the Son carries out the plans, and God the Holy Spirit reveals the plans. Notice that it is singular; there is only *one* Revelation given by Christ, not several, and it was given to John.

Notice the progression of the unveiling; God the Father, to God the Son, to His angel, to the Apostle John, to the bond-servants of Jesus Christ. His bond-servants were under intense persecution at the time it was given so that this book would be a tremendous encouragement to them. *Bond-servant* is from *doulos*, which means a willing slave or servant. God reveals His will to those who want to know and do it.

Soon translates *en tachei*, which literally means "with speed." It can be translated "quickly" as in Revelation. 22:7, 12, and 20, the only three

---

[1] Unless otherwise specified, throughout this study the word(s) following those words being interpreted from the text verses, as here; *the Greek word, apokalupsis*, are references to the *Greek*. The phrase, *the Greek word* is not henceforth included.

other times this phrase occurs in the Book of the Revelation. Some interpret this to mean *soon*, that is, in John's lifetime, and the phrase by itself can mean that. However, all three of the other uses mean that when it happens, it will happen quickly. A third meaning is that *soon* is a relative term, relative to God who is giving this revelation. To Him "a thousand years is as one day."

> But do not let this one fact escape your notice, beloved, that *with the Lord one day is like a thousand years, and a thousand years like one day.* The Lord is not slow about His promise, as some count slowness, but is patient toward you, not wishing for any to perish but for all to come to repentance. [2 Peter 3:8,9].

The Age in which John is living is the Church Age, verse 4, and represents the final age of man, followed by "The Day of the Lord."[2] The Church Age is one of seven Biblical "dispensations," or time periods, in which God deals with man in different ways. However, *the Gospel is the same in every dispensation* (see Genesis 15:6).

This third meaning, ***must shortly take place,*** indicates that this book is prophetic (verse 19), and deals predominantly with the future. Some have said that prophecy is simply pre-written history. Only God knows the future.

His angel is not named, but he could have been Gabriel, who also appeared with important messages to Zechariah in Luke 1:19 ...

> The angel answered and said to him, "I am *Gabriel,* who stands in the presence of God, and I have been *sent to speak to you* and to bring you this good news" (Luke 1:19].

... and Mary in Luke 1:26. Gabriel and Michael are only two of the three angels whose names are given in Scripture.

---

[2] The "Day of the Lord" is a technical phrase that covers the period of time from the day the Church is raptured until the end of the Millennium. See also pages 23, 95, 110, and 177.

But *Michael* the archangel, when he disputed with the devil and argued about the body of Moses, did not dare pronounce against him a railing judgment, but said, "The Lord rebuke you!" [Jude 9].

Satan, also an angel, is often referred to as "Lucifer," assuming that was his name from Isaiah 14:12.

How art thou fallen from heaven, O Lucifer, son of the morning! How thou art cut down to the ground, which didst weaken the nations [Isaiah 14:12 (KJV)].

Here, the King James Version simply transliterates the Hebrew word *Lucifer* into an English word. It is probably a title, correctly translated by the NASV as "star of the morning." Jesus, however, calls him *Satan* in Matthew's Gospel, which is probably the name God gave him after he fell in sin.

Then Jesus said to him, "Go, *Satan!* For it is written, 'you shall worship the Lord your God, and serve Him only' " [Matthew 4:10].

I (Satan) will ascend above the heights of the clouds; I will make myself like the Most High [Isaiah 14:13].

Notice that John could have referred to himself as an "apostle," an authoritative messenger, but he chose rather to call himself a "bond-servant," a *doulos,* a willing slave.

►*[W]ho testified to the word of God and to the testimony of Jesus Christ, even to all that he saw [Revelation 1:2].*

Testified and *testimony* are both from the same Greek word *martureo,* which gives our word *martyr,* someone who bears witness even under the threat of death, and even unto death. *Word* is *logos,* the same word John used in his Gospel in John 1:1 that he later describes in John 1:14-18 as Jesus Christ. *Of Jesus Christ* is another subjective genitive as in verse 1; Jesus is the doer of the action; He is the One who bore witness of God, and John (*he*) bears witness of Christ's witness. *The word of God* pertains to the *character* of Jesus and *the testimony of Jesus Christ* pertains to the *message* of Jesus. John and we today need only bear witness as to who Jesus is and what He says.

> ►*Blessed is he who reads and those who hear the words of the prophecy, and heed the things which are written in it; for the time is near [Revelation 1:3].*

Blessed is *makarios*, which means a supernatural blessing; blessing from God. The Book of the Revelation is the only book of the Bible that offers this promise. This verse could be translated, *Blessed is the one reading and the ones hearing the words of the prophecy and the ones keeping the things having been written in it*. The singular and then plural participles suggest that one person is reading the book (probably in a church gathering), and several persons are listening to the reading.

Hear is *akouo*, which gives the English word "acoustics," and means to hear and take action upon, hence, the third participle *heed*, or "keeping." *Prophecy* is *propheteia*, which in its basic form means a prediction of future events. It also simply means a forthtelling (coming from God, His forthtellings are often of the future). *For the time is near* refers directly to future events.

Time is *kairos*, which in this book refers to a specific time, the time of the end; the first 3 1/2 years of the Tribulation (Revelation 11:18), and the last three and one-half years (Revelation 12:12 and 14).

> And the nations were enraged, and Your wrath came, and *the time came* for the dead to be judged, and the time to reward Your bond-servants the prophets and saints and those who fear Your name, the small and the great, and to destroy those that destroy the earth [Revelation 11:18].

> For this reason, rejoice, O heavens and you that dwell in them. Woe to the earth and the sea, because the devil has come down to you, having great wrath, knowing that he has only a short time .... But the two wings of the great eagle were given to the woman, so that she could fly into the wilderness to her place, where she

was nourished for *a time and times and half a time,* from the presence of the serpent [Revelation 12:12,14].

This interpretation is called *Dispensational,* which uses a literal method of interpretation, and means that God deals with man through specific time periods.[3] The other three methods are called "Allegorical," "Preterite," and "Historical." The *Allegorical* method maintains that the Book of Revelation is only an allegory of stories from which we extract spiritual principles. The *Preterite* method insists that all material contained within the Book was fulfilled in John's day. The *Historical* method defines the book as simply a panorama of the history of the Church.

2. The Salutation or greeting to the churches - Jesus is coming again to rightfully rule on the earth.

> ► *John to the seven churches that are in Asia: Grace to you and peace, from Him who is and who was and who is to come, and from the seven spirits who are before His throne [Revelation 1:4].*

John is the Apostle John introduced first in verse 1. The Revelation is from Jesus Christ to John, but ultimately for the seven churches. *Seven* is the number in Scripture for completion and also the number for perfection. Seven local churches were chosen even though there were more local churches in the province of Asia. "Seven" is used many times in the Book of the Revelation, for example, *seven* seals, *seven* trumpets, *seven* bowls.

Churches is *ekklesiaia,* the plural of *ekklesia,* meaning "the called-out ones," all believers in Christ during the Church Age from Pentecost until the Rapture of the Church.

> I also say to you that you are Peter, and upon this rock I will build My *church,* and the gates of Hades will not overpower it [Matthew 16:18].

---

[3] See Illustration 1

Illustration One – The Seven Dispensations

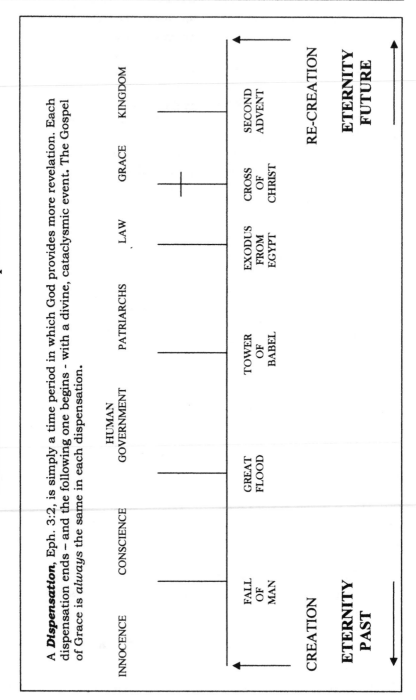

A **Dispensation**, Eph. 3:2, is simply a time period in which God provides more revelation. Each dispensation ends – and the following one begins – with a divine, cataclysmic event. The Gospel of Grace is *always* the same in each dispensation.

INNOCENCE	CONSCIENCE	HUMAN GOVERNMENT	PATRIARCHS	LAW	GRACE	KINGDOM
FALL OF MAN	GREAT FLOOD		TOWER OF BABEL	EXODUS FROM EGYPT	CROSS OF CHRIST	SECOND ADVENT

CREATION

RE-CREATION

ETERNITY PAST

ETERNITY FUTURE

Theologians call *The Church* the "Universal Church," made up of all believers from Pentecost until the Rapture. A local church, then, is the physical manifestation of the Universal Church at any given time in history in any given place. While there can be unbelievers in a local assembly, there are only true believers in the Universal Church because they are supernaturally placed there by the Holy Spirit at the moment of salvation.

> For even as the body is one and yet has many members, and all the members of the body, though they are many, are one body, so also is Christ. For by one Spirit we were all baptized into one body, whether Jews or Greeks, whether slaves or free, and we were all made to drink of one Spirit [1 Corinthians 12:12-13].

The Greek word, *baptizo*, (which we also transliterate into an English word, baptize), means "to identify with by placing into." At the moment of salvation, the Holy Spirit identifies a believer with Christ by "placing him or her into Christ." This is called *Positional Truth* (see Romans 8:1).

These *churches* were in the Roman province of *Asia* located in Southwest Asia Minor. The capital and chief city of this province was Ephesus. Thus, Ephesus receives the first letter, recorded in Chapter 2.

"Grace" is often used of God's attitude toward believers, our standing before Him. **Grace** is *charis*; God's unsought and unmerited favor upon those who deserve exactly the opposite. It also describes God's constant attitude toward believers; once we come under the grace of God through the blood of His Son, we never lose that standing.

> My sheep hear My voice, and I know them, and they follow Me, and I give eternal life to them, and they will never perish; and *no one will snatch them out of My hand.* My Father, who has given them to Me, is greater than all; and *no one is able to snatch them out of the Father's hand.* I and the Father are one [John 10:27-30].

While believers experience God's grace at salvation ...

> For by grace *you have been saved through faith*; and
> that not of yourselves, it is the gift of God; not as a
> result of works, so that no one may boast [Ephesians
> 2:8, 9].

... they never lose the need to experience the grace of God on a daily
basis; hence, John's salutation for God's grace in their lives today.

Peace is *irene*, which gives our English name *Irene*, and which also is
often used of God's daily blessings upon believers as they experience
Him on a daily basis.

Here again, peace is given by God at the moment of our salvation.

> For *He Himself is our peace*, who made both groups
> into one and broke down the barrier of the dividing
> wall [Ephesians 2:14].

But we always need to experience the peace of God in our daily lives.

> [F]or God is not a God of confusion but of peace, as in
> all the churches of the saints [1 Corinthians 14:33].

Although Revelation 1:4-8 briefly introduces us to the seven churches,
the passage really is here to introduce us to God, especially the Lord
Jesus Christ, and why He has a right to rule over the earth. Jesus
rightfully rules because He gives grace and peace and because of the
Essence of God.

While the word *Trinity* does not occur in Scripture, it is a helpful
theological word to describe the fact that the God of the Bible exists in
the form of three Persons, each with all the divine attributes but with
differing ministries. In verses 4b-5a we have a description of the
Trinity:

> ▶ ... *from Him who is and who was and is to come, and*
> *from the seven Spirits who are before His throne, and*
> *from Jesus Christ, the faithful witness, the firstborn of*
> *the dead, and the ruler of the kings of the earth. To*

Him who loves us and released us from our sins by His blood [Revelation 1:4b,5a].

The Father is *Eternal*: *Him* in this context refers to the Father.

Who is and who was and who is to come is a New Testament paraphrase of the Old Testament name for God, *YAHWEH*, which means the eternally Self-existent One. While God bestows His eternal life upon those who trust His Son (John 3:16), only God has always been and will always be.

God said to Moses, "I AM WHO I AM"; and He said, "Thus you shall say to the sons of Israel, 'I AM has sent me to you' " [Exodus 3:14].

▶...*and from the seven spirits who are before His throne [Revelation 1:4c].*

The Spirit is **complete** and **perfect** and **holy**. Again, *seven* is the number of completion and perfection and is the same Spirit of all seven churches.

The seven Spirits who are before His throne is an unusual description of the Holy Spirit. Seven coincides with the seven churches who all have the Spirit, and also represents the completeness and perfection of God. He is Omnipresent and is perfect because He is "before His throne" and only God can dwell in the very presence of God.

a. The Son, Jesus Christ, is the perfect Doer of God's will.

▶ *[A]nd from Jesus Christ ... [Revelation 1:5a].*

Jesus Christ is God the Son, listed last because He is the great theme of this Book of the Revelation.

In verses 5 and 6a John uses two trilogies to describe Christ; three of His Person and three of His accomplishments.

▶ *[A]nd from Jesus Christ, the faithful witness, the firstborn of the dead, and the ruler of the kings of the earth. To Him who loves us and released us from our sins by His blood .... and He has made us to be a kingdom, priests to His God and Father ... [Revelation 1:5, 6a].*

● Of His *Person,* or what He does for God the Father:

(1) The faithful witness.

I have manifested Your name to the men whom You gave Me out of the world; they were Yours and You gave them to Me, and they have kept Your word [John 17:6].

(2) The first-born of the dead.

But now Christ has been raised from the dead, the *first fruits* of those who are asleep [1 Corinthians 15:20].

(3) The ruler of the kings of the earth (see Psalm 2).

● Of His *accomplishments*, or what He does for man:

(1) He loves us.

A new commandment I give to you, that you love one another, even as *I have loved you*, and that you also love one another [John 13:34].

(2) He released us from our sins.

[A]nd He Himself is the *propitiation* for our sins; and not for ours only, but also for those of the whole world [1 John 2:2].

(3) He made us a kingdom and priests to God.

He is *the faithful witness*.

> Now, Father, glorify Me together with Yourself, with the glory which I had with You before the world was. I have manifested Your name to the men whom You gave Me out of the world; they were Yours and You gave them to Me, and they have kept Your word [John 17:5,6].

Faithful is *pistos*, which in the New Testament always has God for its object. We can conclude, then, that Jesus (unlike Satan) always is faithful to God the Father. *Witness*, or "testimony," is from *martureo* (see page 9).

He is the *firstborn of the dead*.

> But now Christ has been raised from the dead, the *first fruits* of those who are asleep [1 Corinthians 15:20].

Firstborn does not refer to generation because Jesus is eternal as is the Father. It refers to being resurrected from the dead. He is the "first fruits" because God is planning a huge harvest of souls of all those who have trusted in His Son as their personal Savior. *The dead*, then, refers only to the "righteous dead ..."

> Then I saw thrones, and they sat on them, and judgment was given to them. And I saw the souls of those who had been beheaded because of their testimony of Jesus and because of the word of God, and those who had not worshipped the beast or his image, and had not received the mark on their forehead and on their hand; and they *came to life* and reigned with Christ for a thousand years [Revelation 20:4].

... not to be confused with the "unrighteous dead."

> The rest of the dead *did not come to life* until the thousand years were completed. [Revelation 20:5].

He is the *ruler of the kings of the earth* (see Psalm 2). Notice the word *and*, which begins this part of the sentence and the period to end it; thus, the trilogy is ended to describe the work of the Son for the Father.

This phrase is actually prophetic, as is Psalm 2, as the Son waits for the Father to make His enemies His footstool.

> Every priest stands daily ministering and offering time after time the same sacrifices, which can never take away sins; but He, having offered one sacrifice for sins for all time, sat down on the right hand of God, waiting from that time onward *until His enemies be made a footstool for His feet* [Hebrews 10:11-13].

This actually occurs in Revelation 19:11ff.

He *loves us*.

> Now before the Feast of the Passover, Jesus knowing that His hour had come that He would depart out of this world to the Father, *having loved His own who were in the world, He loved them to the end* .... A new commandment I give to you, that you love one another, even as *I have loved you*, that you also love one another [John 13:1, 34].

Loves is a present participle expressing continuous action. *Agapao* means unconditional love, the love of choice, the love to the unlovely. This participle is attendant circumstance to the main verb "has made."

He *released us from our sins*.

> [A]nd He Himself is the propitiation for our sins; and for not ours only, but also for those of the whole world [1 John 2:2].

Here is another participle, but this one is aorist denoting completed action; He has *completely released us* from the penalty of our sins.

> Therefore there is now *no condemnation* for those who are in Christ Jesus [Romans 8:1].

> Truly, truly I say to you, he who hears My word, and believes Him who has sent Me, has eternal life, and

does not come into judgment, but has passed out of death into life [John 5:24].

The KJV, based on a more recent Greek text, translates *released,* "washed." That is because the NASV is based on an older Greek text with *lusanti,* meaning to release, while *lousanti* means to wash. The words are pronounced the same and could easily produce an error in transmission of the text. The better text is probably "released."

By His blood shows that salvation is not by works (Ephesians 2:8-9). God is "glorified" because of what Jesus does for us. He has made *us* a kingdom of priests to His God.

> Therefore, since we have a great high priest who has passed through the heavens, Jesus the Son of God, let us hold fast our profession. For we do not have a high priest who cannot sympathize with our weaknesses, but One who has been tempted in all things as we are, yet without sin. Therefore let us draw near with confidence to the throne of grace, so that we may receive mercy and find grace to help in time of need [Hebrews 4:14-16].
>
> ► *[A]nd He has made us to be a kingdom, priests to His God and Father – to Him be the glory and the dominion forever and ever. Amen [Revelation 1:6].*

Has made is an aorist indicative active verb, the main verb of this sentence. It implies completed action - "has made"- we are *already* a kingdom, but without an *established* kingdom on the earth. Our King is ruling upon the throne of God in heaven and has yet to transfer that kingdom to the earth. Also, "we" (the Church Universal), *must not be confused with the kingdom of Israel.*

> So when they had come together, they were asking Him, saying, "Lord, is it at this time You are *restoring the kingdom to Israel?*" [Acts 1:6].

Priests is *hiereis,* the plural of *hiereus,* one who performs sacrificial rites. The adjective means hallowed, holy, divine. *Glory* is *doksa* from *dokeo*, which means to think, to illuminate, to enlighten. ***Dominion*** is *krotos*, meaning dominion, might, strength, power, from the verb *krateo*, which means to be superior, to hold fast, to retain. ***Amen*** is a transliteration of the Greek *amen*, or "so be it," borrowed from the Hebrew *amen*. It carries the idea of the acknowledgement of that which is valid. Jesus will return and rule over the earth.

> ►*Behold, He is coming with the clouds. And every eye will see Him, even those who pierced Him; and all the tribes of the earth will mourn over Him. So it is to be. Amen [Revelation 1:7].*

Clouds refers to the Second Coming of Christ.

> And after He had said these things, He was lifted up while they were looking on, and a *cloud* received Him out of their sight. And as they were gazing intently into the sky while He was going, behold, two men in white clothing stood beside them. They also said, "Men of Galilee, why do you stand looking into the sky? This Jesus who has been taken up from you into heaven, will come in just the same way as you have watched Him go into heaven" [Acts 1:8-11].

He is coming is a first century prediction of the Second Coming of Christ. ***Every eye*** is all people including Jews, ***those who pierced Him...***

> I will pour out on the house of David and on the inhabitants of Jerusalem, the Spirit of grace and of supplication, so that they will look on Me *whom they have pierced*; and they will mourn for Him, as one mourns for an only son, and they will weep bitterly over Him like the bitter weeping over a firstborn [Zechariah 12:10].

... and Gentiles, ***all the tribes of the earth***. They will ***mourn*** because He is coming in judgment.

Verse 8 describes the *eternality* and *omnipotence* of God.

> ▶ *"I am the Alpha and Omega," says the Lord God, "who is and was and who is to come, the Almighty" [Revelation 1:8].*

The first letter of the Greek alphabet is **alpha** and the last letter is **omega,** symbolizing eternality.

B. John saw the resurrected, glorified Jesus Christ (Revelation 1:9-20).

One of the distinguishing characteristics of the apostles of Christ is that they saw and heard the resurrected Christ. Before John was given the message to the churches, he was given a very special revelation; he saw Christ in all His resurrection glory.

1. John heard the voice.

> ▶ *I, John, your brother and fellow partaker in the tribulation and kingdom and perseverance which are in Jesus, was on the island called Patmos because of the word of God and the testimony of Jesus [Revelation 1:9].*

I is a turning point of the first chapter when John begins to refer to himself in the first person. *John* was the beloved disciple, the closest to the Lord Jesus in His earthly ministry. *Brother* is *adelphos*, which is used throughout the New Testament in reference to spiritual brothers. Believers are related in the Body of Christ; they are in the same spiritual family.

Fellow partaker is *sunkoinonos*, "those who fellowship with," or "those who partake together." *Tribulation* is *thlipis*, which literally means pressure, compression; it was used of the Greeks to describe affliction, distress of mind, distressing circumstances, trials and afflictions.

Kingdom is *basileia*, the Kingdom of God, of which all believers in Christ are citizens; we are His ambassadors.

> But seek first His *kingdom* and His righteousness, and all these things will be added to you [Matthew 6:33].

Therefore we are *ambassadors* for Christ, as though God were making an appeal through us; we beg you on behalf of Christ, be reconciled to God [2 Corinthians 5:20].

Perseverance is *hupomone*, which means patient endurance, a patient awaiting, a patient frame of mind, an enduring of affliction. John was on Patmos for about 18 months, banished from being a pastor at Ephesus.

In Jesus is the description of positional truth, of the things that go along with being identified with Christ.

Indeed, all who desire to live godly in Christ Jesus will be persecuted [2 Timothy 3:12].

The island called Patmos is in the South Aegean Sea, just off the coast of Asia Minor. It was where the Roman Emperor Domitian banished certain political prisoners to work the rock quarry. John was probably in his 80's or 90's when banished in A.D. 95 and was allowed to return to Ephesus when Nerva took the throne.

Because introduces why John was there; he was teaching the Word of God and testifying as to who Jesus is.

Testimony is "martureo" (see page 9). *Of Jesus* is an objective genitive; Jesus is the Object of the testimony. Therefore, the Person and work of Jesus is what we should be giving witness to.

▶*I was in the Spirit on the Lord's Day, and I heard behind me a loud voice like the sound of a trumpet [Revelation 1:10].*

I was in the Spirit is a very difficult phrase to translate and to interpret, because "in the Spirit" does not have the definite article and might be translated "in spirit" or "in my spirit" (both with a small "s"), referring to John's human spirit, that immaterial part of man that relates to and communes with the living God. The NASV translators chose to use "the Spirit," referring to the Holy Spirit, who gave John the great vision, or *revelation*, that makes up this great book.

On the Lord's day is usually taken to refer to the first day of the week, however, such references never occur elsewhere in the New Testament (but see Acts 20:7). Or, from historical arguments, some say it refers to Easter Sunday, which is unlikely. Others take this to refer to the Day of the Lord, 2 Peter 3:10, which is also unlikely. "On the Lord's Day" is not the genitive case that would denote possession. It is actually the dative case that could be translated "for the Lord's Day." All 16 of the other New Testament uses translated "Lord's" are in the genitive case.

It might even refer to John being in fellowship and communion with Christ, and so was ready to receive this revelation.

> What was from the beginning, what we have heard, what we have seen with our eyes, what we have looked at and touched with our hands, concerning the Word of Life [1 John 1:1].

A **loud voice** is used to gain attention, as is the use of the trumpet in Scripture.

> As he was traveling, it happened that he was approaching Damascus, and suddenly a light from heaven flashed around him; and he fell to the ground and heard a *voice* saying to him, "Saul, Saul, why are you persecuting me?" And he said, "Who are you Lord?" And He said, "I am Jesus whom you are persecuting, but get up and enter the city, and it will be told you what you must do." The men who traveled with him stood speechless, hearing the *voice* but seeing no one [Acts 9:3-8].

> ▶ *[S]aying, "Write in a book what you see, and send it to the seven churches: to Ephesus and to Smyrna and to Pergamum and to Thyatira and to Sardis and to Philadelphia and to Laodicea" [Revelation 1:11].*

Write resulted in this book becoming part of inspired Scripture.

> All Scripture is *inspired* by God and profitable for teaching, for reproof, for correction, for training in

righteousness; so that the man of God may be adequate, equipped for every good work [2 Timothy 3:16-17].

Book is *biblion* from which we derive the word "Bible," which meant a "scroll" to John. *What you see* means that John would describe in his own words what he saw. That is why the words "like" or "as" occur so many times in this book. *Send it to the seven churches* shows that the Word of God was intended to be shared with God's people. All these local churches were in the province of Asia.

2. John saw Christ glorified.

> ► *Then I turned to see the voice that was speaking with me. And having turned I saw seven golden lampstands [Revelation 1:12].*

I turned to see the voice means that he turned to see the source of the voice. But, the first thing he saw was *seven golden lampstands*. Once again, seven is the number of completion and perfection. *Gold* in Scripture symbolizes Deity. It is impossible to tell if the lampstands had seven sticks as the one in the Temple or just one stick. A little further in the text, verse 20 explains that the lampstands were the seven churches, because a lampstand holds a light that illuminates something or someone. Local churches are to witness for Christ.

> ► *[A]nd in the middle of the lampstands I saw one like a son of man, clothed in a robe reaching to the feet, and girded across His chest with a golden sash [Revelation 1:13].*

In the middle shows that Christ is in the midst of His churches. He knows all about them and their witness. With them is the Divine Presence. *Son of Man* is a common Old and New Testament reference to the Messiah and stresses His humanity.

Clothed in a robe reaching to the feet is literally "clothed to the feet," so we don't know what the robe was like. We do know that the belt or girdle was *golden*, symbolic of the Deity and royalty of the Wearer.

> ▶ *His head and His hair were white like white wool,*
> *like snow; and His eyes were like a flame of fire*
> *[Revelation 1:14].*

White hair was a symbol of purity and glorification, as when Moses in the Old Testament had been in the presence of Deity, his face glowed; Jesus is Deity. These eyes are all-seeing eyes.

Fire is a Scriptural sign of judgment.

> John answered and said to them all, "As for me, I baptize you with water; but One is coming who is mightier than I, and I am not fit to untie the thong of His sandals; He will baptize you with the Holy Spirit and *fire*" [Luke 3:16].

> And the devil who deceived them was thrown into the lake of *fire* and brimstone, where the beast and false prophet are also; and they will be tormented day and night forever and ever [Revelation 20:10].

> ▶ *His feet were like burnished bronze, when it has*
> *been made to glow in a furnace, and His voice was like*
> *the sound of many waters [Revelation 1:15].*

Bronze is the Scriptural symbol for judgment, so wherever Jesus walks He brings judgment or reward, depending on whether the person has trusted Him as Savior or not.

Many waters are overwhelming and overpowering.

> ▶ *In His right hand He held seven stars, and out of His*
> *mouth came a sharp two-edged sword; and His face*
> *was like the sun shining in its strength [Revelation*
> *1:16].*

Right hand is the place of strength, honor, and sovereign possession. *Stars* are *asteros*, from which English derives *asteroid*. *Sword* is *rhomphaia*, found seven times in Scripture (see Revelation 1:16; 2:12, 16; 6:8; 19:15, 21; and Luke 2:35). This was a large, two-edged sword usually wielded with two hands. The *machaira* was a double-edged sword, swung with one hand; made famous by Roman soldiers. The other hand held their shield.

> For the word of God is living and active and sharper than any *two-edged sword*, and piercing as far as the division of soul and spirit, of both joints and marrow, and able to judge the thoughts and intentions of the heart [Hebrews 4:12].

Shining in its strength is Jesus as Lord of Glory, no longer a baby in Bethlehem or the Man of Sorrows.

Christ gave John strength to write.

> ► *When I saw Him, I fell at His feet like a dead man. And He placed His right hand on me saying, "Do not be afraid; I am the first and the last" [Revelation 1:17].*

For *fell at His feet*, see Acts 9 and John 11. It is the normal response of a mortal in the presence of Deity. *Right hand* is the symbol of strength.

Do not be afraid starts a quote of Jesus that continues through Chapter three. John was probably afraid that he might die because he saw God's unveiled glory.

> So Manoah said to his wife, "*We will surely die*, for we have seen God" [Judges 13:22].

I am the first and the last refers to Christ's Eternality, Sovereignty, Deity and Creatorship.

> ► *[A]nd the living One; and I was dead, and behold I am alive forevermore, and I have the keys of death and Hades [Revelation 1:18].*

The living One equals eternally self-existent.

I was dead, and behold I am alive forevermore refers to *Atonement Theology*. Sins *must* be covered with blood. For us to be saved required the death of Christ.

> And according to the Law, one may almost say, all things are *cleansed with blood*, and without shedding of blood, there is no forgiveness [Hebrews 9:22].

"Atonement" means a *covering*. Man tries to cover his sin but cannot. Therefore, God, who could not experience death, became a man, the Lord Jesus Christ, so He could have blood, shed that blood, experience death, and provide the "covering" for the sins of the human race. Now, Jesus is "alive forevermore."

Keys are symbolic of authority. *Death and Hades* refer to both the people who are dead and the place where they are. *These dead people do not cease to exist.*

> ► *Therefore write the things which you have seen, and the things which are, and the things which will take place after these things [Revelation 1:19].*

This verse gives the broad outline to the Book of the Revelation:[4]

... *the things which you have seen*, Chapter 1.
... *the things which are*, Chapters 2-3.
... *the things which shall take place after these things*, Chapters 4-22.

> ► *As for the mystery of the seven stars which you saw in My right hand, and the seven golden lampstands: the seven stars are the angels of the seven churches, and the seven lampstands are the seven churches [Revelation 1:20].*

Mystery is *musterion*, which is something hidden that must be revealed.

Angels is *angellos*, which means a "messenger" (see also page 29).

---

[4] See Illustration 2.

Illustration Two – The Chapters of The Revelation

4-5

RAPTURE

SECOND
ADVENT

1   2-3

6

7

10-14

17-18

8-9   15-16

19   20   21-22

CHURCH
AGE

TRIBULATION

KINGDOM AGE
(MILLENNIUM)

II. **Present** - "write the things which are," Chapters 2 and 3.

Chapters 2 and 3 consist of the seven letters to the seven churches that existed in John's day in the Province of Asia, located in the southwest corner of Asia Minor.[5] Today it is Turkey. It can be illustrated that the various characteristics of these seven churches of John's day parallel those that have existed throughout the Church Age right up until the time when Jesus will return. Every local assembly in every generation can learn from these letters.

A. The letter to Ephesus – Theme of the letter: let love be the real motivation behind your service for Christ, Revelation 2:1-7.

1.   The Destination - the church in Ephesus.

> ▶ *To the angel of the church in Ephesus write: [Revelation 2:1].*

Angel is *angelos*, which simply means *messenger*. In the Book of the Revelation *angels* probably refers to angelic beings; perhaps a special holy angel is assigned to each local church. It seems to be used in the text 67 times for angelic beings and nine other times for human messengers, and it is used in Luke 9:52 and James 2:25 for human beings.

> [A]nd he sent *messengers* on ahead of him, and they went and entered a village of the Samaritans to make arrangements for him [Luke 9:52].

> In the same way, was not Rahab the harlot also justified by works when she received the *messengers* and sent them out by another way? [James 2:25].

Church is *ekklasia*, which means *called out ones*. Believers are called out of the world for special, holy purposes, at least to preach the Gospel and to live the Gospel. *Ephesus* was the largest of the seven cities, having a population of about 600,000 and was the capital city of the

---

[5] See Illustration 3

Illustration Three; The Seven Letters to the Churches

Church	Commendation	Rebuke	Exhortation
Ephesus	For persevering in godly deeds	For leaving their first love	To repent and return to a motive of love
Smyrna	For their perseverance under persecution	None given	Not to fear, but be faithful unto death
Pergamum	For their faithfulness to Christ	They have not held on to pure doctrine	Repent and purge their church of false teaches
Thyatira	For their sincere, increasing service to the Lord	For compromising their Christian principles	To hold fast to an uncompromising position
Sardis	None given	For being a spiritually dead church	To wake up and finish the work
Philadelphia	For being faithful to Christ and the Word of God	None given	To hold fast until Jesus comes
Laodicea	None given	For being lukewarm	To repent and be zealous for good works

Province of Asia. It was a very wicked city, filled with idolatry (see Acts 18:23-19:41).

Write is *grapho*, which gives our word *graphic*.

2. The Commendation - for persevering in Godly deeds.

> ► *The One who holds the seven stars in His right hand, the One who walks among the seven golden lampstands, says this [Revelation 2:1b].*

The One is the resurrected, glorified Jesus Christ (see Revelation 1:13-15). **Holds** is *kraton* (the same as in Revelation 1:16), which means "to hold with authority."

Once again, **Seven** is the number of completion, the number of perfection. Notice that this description of Christ was used in Chapter 1, verses 13 and 16. Each letter in Chapters two and three includes part of the description of Christ from the first chapter. Each part is significant to the letter; so this one stresses His authority and omnipresence. Jesus is with every local church and knows everything about them.

Right hand is the place of strength, honor, power, and sovereign possession. **Walks** is *peripateo*, which means to walk around, a description of life-style. Revelation 1:20 says **stars** are the angels of the churches, and the **lampstands** are the churches. **Says** is the main verb and **who holds** and **who walks** are both present participles of attendant circumstance that lend credence to what He says.

> ► *I know your deeds and your toil and perseverance, and that you cannot tolerate evil men, and you put to the test those who call themselves apostles and they are not, and you found them to be false [Revelation 2:2].*

I know is from *oida*, which means to know by observation. This knowledge is the result of His Omnipresence in verse 1b. **Deeds** is *erga*, from *energo*, from which we derive "energy." It recurs in verse five. **Toil** is *kopiao*, which means to work so hard as to work up a sweat.

Perseverance is *hupomone,* meaning patient endurance and persistence. It speaks of waiting on the Lord for deliverance. *Tolerate* is *bastazo,* which means to lift up, to carry, to endure. Seen again in verse 3, this tolerance also speaks of waiting upon God to vindicate His people.

Evil men is all one word in the Greek and reminds us that Satan uses people in local churches to accomplish his evil deeds. *Put to the test* is *pirazo,* which means to test so as to approve (aorist tense denotes completed action). *Call themselves* shows that their authority had not come from Christ.

Jesus hand-picked every one of His Apostles.

> Jesus *summoned* His twelve disciples and gave them authority over unclean spirits, to cast them out, and to heal every kind of disease and every kind of sickness. Now the names of the twelve apostles are these ... [Matthew 10:1,2a].

An apostle, *apostolos,* was one sent with the authority of the sender, with a special message. *False* is *pseudeis,* which gives our word *pseudo.* They were tested and found to be false because *their doctrine was false!*

> ▸ *[A]nd you have perseverance and have endured for My name's sake, and have not grown weary [Revelation 2:3].*

You have endured is aorist tense, completed action; they had endured up until now. *For My name's sake* describes the reason why they persevered and endured; for Christ's sake. Matthew 7:21-23 illustrates how unbelievers can use the power of Christ's name to do good works.

> Not everyone who says to Me, "Lord, Lord" will enter into the kingdom of heaven, but he who does the will of My Father who is in heaven will enter. Many will say to Me on that day, "Lord, Lord, did we not *prophesy in Your name,* and *in Your name cast out demons,* and *in Your name perform many miracles?*" And then I will declare to them, "I never knew you,

depart from Me, you who *practice lawlessness"* [Matthew 7:21-23].

Have not grown weary could be translated "have not given up." They received an A+ for endurance!

1. The Rebuke - for leaving their first love.

    ▶ *But I have this against you, that you have left your first love [Revelation 2:4].*

But is *alla,* a strong contrasting conjunction. ***You have left*** is another aorist tense, denoting completed action, from *aphiemi,* which means to depart. The active voice means they *chose* to do this. ***First love*** was Christ Himself. Here, "love" is *agape,* which is unconditional love, that love of a believer for his/her Savior.

2. The Exhortation - to repent, return to a motive of love.

    ▶ *Therefore remember from where you have fallen, and repent and do the deeds you did at first; or else I am coming to you and will remove your lampstand out of its place – unless you repent. Yet this you do have, that you hate the deeds of the Nicolaitans, which I also hate [Revelation 2:5,6].*

Therefore introduces a conclusion; after Christ's rebuke in verse 4, there should come a searching for what God wants them to do. ***Remember*** is *mnamoneuo,* from which we derive *memory.* ***You have fallen*** is another aorist tense.

Repent is imperative mood, the mood of command. It, too, is aorist tense. The verb is *metanoeo,* which is made up of *meta* meaning with, and *noeo,* meaning the mind. "With the mind" to a Greek meant to *change the mind* to agree with another idea. Context must decide what must be changed. For example, in the book of Acts, the Jews must change their minds about who Jesus is - their Messiah - whom they had turned over to the Romans to be nailed to the cross.

Peter said to them, "repent ..." [Acts 2:38a].

In Hebrews there is a *change of mind* about dead works.

> Therefore leaving the elementary teaching about the Christ, let us press on to maturity, not laying again a foundation of *repentance* from dead works and of faith toward God [Hebrews 6:1].

Works do not produce salvation, so people need to *change their minds* about this. In Revelation 9:20-21 evil men refused to change their minds about performing evil deeds that would only lead them to judgment. Repentance does not require a deep emotional experience, but it can include it. *Do the deeds you did at first* to Christ are different deeds than the ones done after they left their first love. He sees them differently because they changed their motivation.

Or else introduces the Divine discipline that Jesus will exercise if they refuse to repent. Jesus has authority to discipline His local churches.

> And Jesus came up and spoke to them, saying, "All authority has been given to Me in heaven and on earth" [Matthew 28:18].

History tells us the church at Ephesus did repent and Jesus went on to use them for a long time. *I will remove your lampstand*, means that He will remove their testimony of Him.

History says that the *Nicolaitans* held that it was lawful to eat things offered to idols, and to mix in and even encourage the worship of idols. They denied God to be the Creator of the world, ascribing its existence to other powers. They were a licentious people.[6]

5. The Promise - to bring overcomers to Paradise.

> ▶ *He who has an ear, let him hear what the Spirit says to the churches. To him who overcomes, I will grant to eat of the tree of life which is in the paradise of God [Revelation 2:7].*

---

[6] Merrill F. Unger, *Unger's New Bible Dictionary*, 3rd Ed.,7th Printing (Chicago: Moody Bible Institute) p. 792.

He who has an ear is a way of saying that the listener has a responsibility to respond to the message. *Hear* is *akouo*, which means to hear with a response. *The Spirit* is the Holy Spirit, who inspired the writing of the Bible.

> But know this first of all, that no prophecy of Scripture is a matter of one's own interpretation, for no prophecy was ever made by an act of human will, but men *moved by the Holy Spirit spoke from God* [2 Peter 1:20, 21].

To the churches shows that this letter is to eventually be read to all the churches in Asia. *Him who overcomes* is a believer in Christ.

> For whatever is born of God overcomes the world; and this is the victory that has overcome the world – our faith. Who is the one who overcomes the world, but *he who believes* that Jesus is the Son of God? [1 John 5:4, 5].

Eat of the tree of life is a way to describe eternal life.

> Then he showed me a river of the water of life, clear as crystal, coming from the throne of God and of the Lamb, in the middle of its street. On either side of the river was the tree of life, bearing twelve kinds of fruit, yielding its fruit every month; and the leaves of the tree were for the healing of the nations [Revelation 22:1,2 (see also Genesis 2:9, 16-17; 3:1-7, 22-24)].

Paradise is *paradise*, meaning a "pleasure park," usually with all sorts of trees and usually stocked with wild game for hunting. *Of God* is a genitive of possession.

B. The letter to Smyrna – Theme of the letter: keep persevering through the trials of life, Revelation 2:8-11.

1. The Destination - the church in Smyrna.

▶ *And to the angel of the church in Smyrna write [Revelation 2:8a].*

For *angel, church, and write,* see pages 29, 31.

Smyrna was a very beautiful and influential city 40 miles north of Ephesus in the Province of Asia. It had a population of 200,000 and was referred to as the "First of Asia," referring to its beauty. It was built on the top of a hill, making the skyline look like a crown. It was a wealthy city where the sciences and medicine flourished. Always siding with Rome, Smyrna earned special privileges as a free, self-governing city. The "Golden Street" had temples to Zeus and Cybele at either end and along the street were temples to Apollo, Asclepius and Aphrodite. Smyrna was the center of emperor worship, building the first temple to Tiberius Caesar.

Under Emperor Domitian, A.D. 81-96, emperor worship became mandatory requiring citizens to throw a pinch of incense onto the altar to the godhead of Caesar while saying, "Caesar is Lord." Upon this annual act of worship, a certificate was awarded which said, "We, the representatives of the Emperor, Serenos and Hermas, have seen you sacrificing." Consequently, persecution of Christians in Smyrna was very intense when they refused to worship Caesar. For refusing, one bishop in A.D. 155 named Polycarp was burned at the stake, the twelfth to suffer public execution under the persecution of Emperor Adrian.[7]

---

[7] He stepped forward, and was asked by the proconsul if he really was Polycarp. When he said yes, the proconsul urged him to deny the charge. "Respect your years!" he exclaimed, adding similar appeals regularly made on such occasions: "Swear by Caesar's fortune; change your attitude; say: 'Away with the Godless!' " But Polycarp, with his face set, looked at all the crowd in the stadium and waved his hand toward them, sighed, looked up to heaven, and cried: "Away with Godless!" The governor pressed him further: "Swear, and I will set you free: execrate Christ." "For eighty-six years," replied Polycarp, "I have been His servant, and He has never done me wrong: how can I blaspheme my King who saved me?" "I have wild beasts," said the proconsul. "I shall throw you to them, if you don't change your attitude."

"Call them," replied the old man. "We cannot change our attitude if it means a change from better to worse. But it is a splendid thing to change from cruelty to justice." "If you make light of the beasts," retorted the governor, "I'll have you destroyed by fire, unless you change your attitude." Polycarp answered: "The fire you threaten burns for a time and is soon extinguished: there is a fire you know nothing about – the fire of the judgment to come and of eternal punishment, the fire reserved for the ungodly. But

2. The Commendation - for their perseverance under persecution.

> ▶ *The first and the last, who was dead, and has come to life, says this [Revelation 2:8b].*

The first and the last (compare Revelation 1:17-18, page 26), includes the attributes of Christ as Eternal, Creator, Sovereign, and Deity. Thus, the suffering and persecution experienced by any Christian in any age is under God's permissive will. ***Who was dead*** is literally "who became dead;" this shows the ability of Christ to identify with anyone who is suffering, because He Himself suffered greatly.

And has come to life shows God's ultimate victory over all suffering of His children.

> But Abraham said, "Child, remember that during your life you received your good things, and likewise Lazarus bad things; but now *he is being comforted* here..."[Luke 16:25a].

Says this is present tense, emphasizing the authority and present relevance of the Word of God.

> ▶ *I know your tribulation and your poverty (but you are rich) and the blasphemy by those who say they are*

---

why do you hesitate? Do what you want." The proconsul was amazed and sent the crier to stand in the middle of the arena and announce three times:

"Polycarp has confessed that he is a Christian." Then a shout went up from every throat that Polycarp must be burnt alive...the rest followed in less time than it takes to describe: the crowds rushed to collect logs and faggots from workshop and public baths...When the pyre was ready...Polycarp prayed: "Oh, Father of Thy beloved and blessed Son, Jesus Christ, through whom we have come to know Thee, and God of angels and powers and all creation, and of the whole family of the righteous who live in Thy presence; I bless Thee for counting me worthy of this day and hour, that in the number of the martyrs I may partake of Christ's cup, to the resurrection of eternal life of both soul and body in the imperishability that is the gift of the Holy Spirit...."

When he had offered up the Amen and completed his prayer, the men in charge lit the fire, and a great flame shot up. *Eusebius*, History of the Church, IV 15.

*Jews and are not, but are a synagogue of Satan
[Revelation 2:9]*

For *I know*, see page 31.

Tribulation is *thlipsis,* the same in verse 10 and Revelation 1:9. *Poverty* is *ptocheian,* which was the Greek word for abject poverty. Evidently, the persecution of Christians in Smyrna was through economic pressure. *But you are rich* gives God's point of view of their situation: He looks upon His children from a spiritual perspective.

God is *Spirit,* and those who worship Him must
worship in *Spirit* and truth [John 4:24].

Blasphemy is the Greek *blasphemia,* which means a railing, a reproach, an evil speaking. *Say they are Jews and are not* means they are not the spiritual recipients of the Abrahamic promises, because they have rejected Christ. (See John 8:31-47, in particular, vv. 33 and 44.)

Synagogue is from *sunagoga,* which means an assembly of people, a gathering place. Notice the singular, "*a* synagogue," teaches that not *all* synagogues are bad. *Satan* is *satan,* meaning adversary, opponent, enemy.

3. The Rebuke - none given. The intense persecution of these Christians in Smyrna was probably the contributing factor that produced their purity. Because of the persecution, Christ had nothing about which to rebuke them for.

4. The Exhortation - Do not fear but be faithful unto death.

▶ *Do not fear what you are about to suffer. Behold the
devil is about to cast some of you into prison, so that
you will be tested, and you will have tribulation for ten
days. Be faithful until death, and I will give you the
crown of life [Revelation 2:10].*

Do not fear is present imperative middle. Present tense could be translated "stop being afraid." Imperative mood is the mood of command. Fear is a feeling, but God can command us to change our feelings. Middle voice expresses something that the subject does to himself that benefits himself.

> I say to you, My friends, *do not be afraid* of those who can kill the body and after that have no more that they can do. But I will warn you who to fear: *fear the One* who, after He has killed, has authority to cast into hell; yes, I tell you, *fear Him*! [Luke 12:4,5].

To suffer is *pascho*, which means to be affected by something (whether good or bad), to suffer, to endure evil. *Pascho* is possibly borrowed from the Hebrew *pesach*, which referred to the Passover. This word carries the idea of suffering (in sacrifice). The sacrificial lamb of the Passover can be called the "Paschal Lamb." In an absolute sense without case or adjunct it refers to death, used at least 13 times this way in reference to the death of Christ. Hence, here it probably carries the idea of ensuing death. *Devil* is *diabolos*, which means an accuser, or slanderer (Revelation 12:10).

> ... now the salvation, and the power, and the kingdom of our God and the authority of His Christ have come, for the *accuser* of our brethren has been thrown down, he who *accuses* them before our God day and night [Revelation 12:10b].

Into prison in the ancient world was where a person was kept when accused of a crime until his trial.

> [F]or which I am an ambassador *in chains*; that in proclaiming it I might speak boldly, as I ought to speak [Ephesians 6:20].

Tested is *pierazo*, the same as in Revelation 2:2, which can mean to test so as to approve. This testing, trial, or tribulation, is to provide an opportunity to glorify God.

Be faithful until death probably comes at the end of the literal *ten days*. *I will give you* shows the power and authority of Jesus Christ. *Crown* is *stephanos*, which was an earned crown, and is never used in the New Testament for salvation, but only for rewards to believers. The crown of life will be awarded by Christ to those who have endured suffering.[8]

> Blessed is a man who perseveres under trial; for once he has been approved, he will receive the *crown of life* which the Lord has promised to those who love Him [James 1:12].

5. The Promise - to protect overcomers from the Second Death.

> ▶ *He who has an ear let him hear what the Spirit says to the churches. He who overcomes will not be hurt by the second death [Revelation 2:11].*

For **Hear, the Spirit, churches**, and **overcomes** see page 35.

The second death is eternal separation from the presence of God and being under the wrath of God in the Lake of Fire forever.

> Blessed and holy is the one who has a part in the first resurrection; over these the *second death* has no power, but they will be priests of God and of Christ and will reign with Him for a thousand years .... Then Death and Hades were thrown into the lake of fire. This is the *second death*, the lake of fire [Revelation 20:6, 14].

> But for the cowardly and unbelieving and abominable and murderers and immoral persons and sorcerers and idolaters and all liars, their part will be in the lake that burns with fire and brimstone, which is the *second death* [Revelation 21:8]

---

[8] Why Christians suffer:
• Because of corrective Divine discipline, see Hebrews 12:1-11.
• Because of preventive Divine discipline, see 2 Corinthians 12:7.
• Because Christians need to grow spiritually, see James 1:1-12.
• Because the suffering of Christians sometimes glorifies God, see 1 Peter 4:7-19.
• Because Christians are caught in the Angelic Conflict, see Job Chapters 1-42.
• Because the suffering of Christians spreads the gospel, see Philippians 1:12-30
• Because Christians learn how to comfort suffering people, see 2 Corinthians 1:1-11.

Then He will also say to those on His left, "Depart from Me, accursed ones, into the *eternal fire* which has been prepared for the devil and his angels .... These will go away into *eternal punishment*, but the righteous into eternal life [Matthew 25:41, 46].

C. The letter to Pergamum – Theme of the letter: keep your doctrine pure, Revelation 2:12-17.

1. The Destination - the church in Pergamum.

> ▶ *And to the angel at Pergamum write [Revelation 2:12a].*

For *angel* and *write*, see pages 29 and 31.

Pergamum was a very significant city 65 miles north along the fertile valley of the Caicus River. It was prosperous, with a large library of 200,000 volumes, second only to the library at Alexandria in North Africa. It had a famous hospital dedicated to Asclepius, the savior god of healing, represented by the serpent. On the crest of the hill was a great altar to Soter Zeus (or "savior Zeus," the chief god of the Greeks), which Christians referred to as the throne of Satan. The city had temples to Dionysus, Athena, Asclepius, and Demeter, and three temples to the emperor cult, making it a very dangerous place to live as a Christian, especially when persecution came down from the emperor himself.

2. The Commendation - for their faithfulness to Christ.

> ▶ *The One who has the sharp two-edged sword says this [Revelation 2:12b].*

The One is Jesus Christ who is described in detail in Chapter one. The *sharp two-edged sword*, cf. Revelation 1:16, was the *romphaia*, a long, two-handed, double-edged sword designed to yield fatal blows with one swing. The sword represents the Word of God and its power (Revelation 19:15, 21), and its two edges represent its power to either cut the chains of sin that bind a *repentant* sinner or pronounce judgment upon a *unrepentant* sinner ...

> Truly, truly, I say to you, he who hears My word, and believes on Him that sent me, has eternal life, and does not come into judgment, but has passed out of death into life [John 5:24].

... or to judge a Christ-rejecting sinner.

> From His mouth comes a sharp *sword*, so that with it He may strike down the nations, and He will rule them with a rod of iron; and He treads the wine press of the fierce wrath of God, the Almighty .... And the rest were killed with the *sword* which came from the mouth of Him who sat on the horse, and all the birds were filled with their flesh [Revelation 19:15, 21].

> ► *I know where you dwell, where Satan's throne is; and you hold fast My name, and did not deny My faith even in the days of Antipas, My witness, My faithful one, who was killed among you, where Satan dwells [Revelation 2:13].*

For *I know*, see page 31. **Satan's throne** was the great altar to Soter Zeus, the chief god and savior of the Greeks. Some of the believers in the church at Pergamum did two things well: they **held fast His name**, and they **did not deny His faith**. *My* refers to Jesus Christ. *Name* refers to a *whole* person, who he is, what he stands for, his character, integrity and reputation.

Faith is a body of doctrine, "which was once for all handed down to the saints."

> Beloved, while I was making every effort to write you about our common salvation, I felt the necessity to write to you appealing that you contend earnestly for the faith which was once for all *handed down to the saints* [Jude 3].

Antipas, the bishop of Pergamum, was martyred under the persecution of Domitian, the same emperor who banished John to Patmos.

Tradition says the priests of Asclepius put Antipas in a brazen bull and roasted him alive.

Christ calls Antipas *My witness* (Greek *martureo*, English "martyr"), and *My faithful one*, which John used to describe Jesus in Revelation 1:5.

3. The Rebuke - You have not held on to pure doctrine.

> ► *But I have a few things against you, because you have there some who hold the teaching of Balaam, who kept teaching Balak to put a stumbling block before the sons of Israel, to eat things sacrificed to idols and to commit acts of immorality [Revelation 2:14].*

But is *alla*, a very strong conjunction of contrast. *You have there some* shows that the believers in the church at Pergamum were now allowing false teachers to remain in the church and practice and teach their false doctrine. *The teaching of Balaam* is explained partially in the rest of the verse, *to eat things sacrificed to idols, and to commit acts of immorality.* These two things usually went together in the ancient world. Chapters 22-25 and 31:15-16 of the book of Numbers describe how Satan used Balaam to seduce God's people into unlawful, mixed marriages which led them into idolatry and sexual immorality. The Christians in Pergamum were falling into the same trap. Historically, there is a recurring cycle in the Church; first, there is a softening of Biblical doctrine, then there is a merging of Biblical doctrine and pagan philosophy, and finally there is moral corruption of the people themselves.

> ► *So you also have some who in the same way hold the teaching of the Nicolaitans [Revelation 2:15].*

Some .... hold the teaching of the Nicolaitans, which Jesus said in Revelation 2:6 that He hated. It was basically a doctrine of license, a misuse and abuse of God's grace.

> What then? Shall we sin because we are not under the law but under grace? May it never be! [Romans 6:15].

Interestingly, the Hebrew word *balaam* and the Greek word *nicolas* both mean the same thing; "to conquer the people." Satan's plan has always been to use evil men to conquer God's people, either Israel or the Church.

4. The Exhortation - To repent and purge the church of false teachers.

> ▶ *Therefore repent, or else I am coming to you quickly, and I will make war against them with the sword of My mouth [Revelation 2:16].*

Repent is *metanoeo,* which means to change the mind (which will result in a change of behavior). Context must determine if "repent" applies to believers or unbelievers. See also page 33.

Therefore introduces the result of the rebuke from verses 14-15. *I am coming to you quickly* would probably be in the form of apostles coming with authoritative doctrine and extreme church discipline.

> If your brother sins, go and show him his fault in private; if he listens to you, you have won your brother. But if he does not listen to you, take one or two more with you, so that by the mouth of two or three witnesses every fact may be confirmed. If he refuses to listen to them, tell it to the church; and if he refuses to listen even to the church, let him be to you as a Gentile and a tax collector [Matthew 18:15-17].

> ... those who cause dissensions ... *turn away from them* [Romans 16:17].

> I wrote you in my letter *not to associate with* immoral people [1 Corinthians 5:9].

> But actually, I wrote to you *not to associate with* any so-called brother if he is an immoral person ... [1 Corinthians 5:11a].

> ... *Remove* the wicked man from among yourselves [1 Corinthians 5:13].

Now we command you brethren, in the name of our Lord Jesus Christ, that you *keep away from* every brother who leads an unruly life and not according to the tradition which you received from us [2 Thessalonians 3:6].

And if anyone does not obey our instruction in this letter ... *do not associate with* him, so that he may be put to shame. Yet do not regard him as an enemy, but admonish him as a brother [2 Thessalonians 3:14,15].

Reject a factious man after a first and second warning, knowing that such a man is perverted and is sinning, being self-condemned [Titus 3:10,11].

Them refers to the Balaamites and Nicolaitans of verses 14 and 15. **The sword of My mouth** is the Word of God.

5. The Promise - Christ will eternally provide for all overcomers.

▶ *He who has an ear, let him hear what the Spirit says to the churches. To him who overcomes, to him I will give some of the hidden manna, and I will give him a white stone, and a new name written on the stone which no one knows but he who receives it [Revelation 2:17].*

For **hear, Spirit, churches,** and **overcomes**, see page 35. **The hidden manna** was "hidden" in the Ark of the Covenant, representing Jesus Christ as the Bread of Life.

Jesus said to them, I am the *bread of life*, he who comes to Me will not hunger, and he who believes in Me will never thirst [John 6:35].

This manna, which was God's miraculous provision for His people in the wilderness is also "hidden" from the world of unbelievers.

But a natural man does not accept the things of the Spirit of God, for they are *foolishness* to him; and he cannot understand them, because they are spiritually appraised [1 Corinthians 2:14].

But He answered and said, "For it is written, man shall not live by bread alone, but on *every word* that proceeds out of the mouth of God" [Matthew 4:4].

A *white stone* was sometimes used as an invitation to a banquet; but it was also used in legal matters, given to an acquitted person to be worn as an amulet around the neck to publicly show the person is innocent of all charges. Probably both images are in view here; it is Christ's personal invitation to every believer to the Marriage Supper of the Lamb, and it is an amulet to be worn in heaven by forgiven sinners.

A new name will either be the name of Christ Himself (Revelation 19:12), or a brand new name for each glorified believer. In eternity, God can give every redeemed sinner a separate name. While the courts of this earth may condemn us and put us to physical death, God invites us to live with Him in heaven forever!

D. The letter to Thyatira – Theme of the letter: serve Christ without compromising, Revelation 2:18-29.

1. The Destination - The church at Thyatira.

> ► *And to the angel at Thyatira write ... [Revelation 2:18a].*

For *angel* and *write*, see pages 29 and 31.

Thyatira was a small, but prosperous town located about 40 miles southeast of Pergamum. It was an older city, having been established by Alexander the Great as a Macedonian colony. Being located in a rich agricultural area, Thyatira was famous for its manufacture of purple dye, wool, linen, apparel, leatherwork, tanning, and excellent bronze work. Secular writings refer several times to the trade guilds and network of unions of this city. The worship of Apollo, the sun god, and Artemis (or Diana, the goddess of fertility), was prominent. Each trade guild had its own patron deity, feasts, and seasonal festivities that included sexual immorality. Acts 16:14 mentions Lydia, a seller of purple fabrics, as being from Thyatira. Acts 19:10 suggests that the church was founded here while Paul was in Ephesus.

2. The Commendation - for their sincere, increasing service to the Lord.

> ► *The Son of God, who has eyes like a flame of fire, and His feet are like burnished bronze, says this [Revelation 2:18b].*

The Son of God title for Christ is found only here in the Book of the Revelation. While *Son of Man* (Revelation 1:13), stresses His humanity, *Son of God* stresses His Deity. The *eyes* depict the righteous discernment of Christ since *the flame of fire* tests metal to show its quality. *Feet* is used in Scripture to represent judgment,

> [A]nd they will fall by the edge of the sword, and will be led captive into all the nations; and Jerusalem will be *trampled under foot* by the Gentiles until the times of the Gentiles are fulfilled [Luke 21:24.].

Burnished bronze translates *chalkolibano*, only here and Revelation 1:15 in the New Testament. It was a factitious or man-made alloy of brass rich in zinc, which would astonish the bronze workers of Thyatira.

> *I know your deeds, and your love and faith and service and perseverance, and that your deeds of late are greater than at first [Revelation 2:19].*

For *I know* see page 31. Christ "knows" and commends them for five things of which their "deeds" have increased. For *deeds* see page 31. *Love* is *agape*, the love of choice, which the Ephesians were lacking. So, these Christians of Thyatira were sincere.

Faith is *pistis*, which has God as its object in the New Testament. ***Service*** is *diakonia*, from which we derive "deacon," a servant in the church. For ***perseverance*** see pages 22 and 32.

3. The Rebuke - for compromising their Christian principles.

47

> ▶ *But I have this against you, that you tolerate the woman Jezebel, who calls herself a prophetess, and she teaches and leads My bond-servants astray so that they commit acts of immorality and eat things sacrificed to idols [Revelation 2:20].*

But, see page 33. *This* is in italics in the NASV. The KJV reads, "a few things" (plural). The elipsis probably denotes a singular thing Christ has against them, namely, their compromise to the teachings of Jezebel. *Tolerate* is *aphiami*, an aorist participle attending "have against." *Aphiami* is *apo*, meaning apart, apart from, against, plus *histami*, which means to stand; hence, to stand apart or send away or send forth. It came to mean to allow to stand apart, to let alone, to relax, to pardon, to be less intense. Usually, it is translated "forgive."

Jezebel is probably a *title* after 1 Kings 21:1-23, and not the actual name of the woman. (Notice that no one has named a daughter Jezebel since 1 Kings 21.) *Calls herself* shows her arrogance even though a "prophetess" (Greek, *prophetis*) was a valid New Testament spiritual gift.

> Now this man had four virgin daughters who were *prophetesses* [Acts 21:9].

Teaches (*didasko*) and *leads astray* (*plano*) are both present indicative verbs. *Plano* means to deceive (Revelation 20:10); it is what the devil does.

Bond-servants is *doulos*, which is a willing slave. *Commit acts of immorality* is from *porneia*, from which we derive "pornography." *Things sacrificed to idols* is *eidolothuta*. Both these acts were part of the regular pagan festivities. Jezebel was teaching a brand of licentiousness similar to that practiced by the Nicolaitans.

> ▶ *I gave her time to repent, and she does not want to repent of her immorality [Revelation 2:21].*

I gave her time to repent is pure grace on God's part.

The Lord is not slow about His promise, as some count slowness, but is patient toward you, not wishing for any to perish but for all to come to repentance [2 Peter 3:9].

For *Repent*, see page 33. *She does not want* shows the function of the human will.

> ▶ Behold, I will throw her on a bed of sickness, and those who commit adultery with her into great tribulation, unless they repent of her deeds [Revelation 2:22].

I will throw is a present tense translated by what we call a futuristic present. It translates as future, but has the impact of the immediate present, "I cast," as if it is imminent. *A bed* is where she committed immorality, so Christ *will throw her upon a bed of sickness. Adultery* is used only here in the seven letters, indicating a worse situation at Thyatira than in the other churches. Notice that Christ had not become angry at their sin, but at their refusal to repent.

> ▶ And I will kill her children with pestilence, and all the churches will know that I am He who searches the minds and hearts; and I will give to each one of you according to your deeds [Revelation 2:23].

Her children probably refers to her followers; see *those who commit adultery with her*, verse 22. *Will know* is *ginosko*, which means to know by experience, to know first hand; it is the same in verse 24. *All the churches will know* is part of the reason for Divine discipline and Christ's warning.

Minds is *nephros*, the Greek word for kidneys, which gave that deep, physical feeling from man's soul, or conscience. *I will give to each one of you according to your deeds* shows that Christ knows the deeds of each individual in each church.

4. The Exhortation - to hold fast to an uncompromising position.

> ▶ *But I say to you, the rest who are in Thyatira, who do not hold this teaching, who have not known the deep things of Satan, as they call them – I place no other burden on you [Revelation 2:24].*

The rest is the remnant within the remnant; the small group of Christians who refused to follow Jezebel. **The deep things of Satan** are in contrast to "the deep things of God."

> For to us God revealed them through the Spirit; for the Spirit searches all things, even the *depths of God* [1 Corinthians 2:10].

> ▶ *Nevertheless what you have, hold fast until I come [Revelation 2:25].*

Hold fast was an unswerving refusal to compromise. **Until I come** is the first reference in the seven letters to the Rapture of the Church.

5. The Promise - to rule with Christ when He returns.

> ▶ *He who overcomes, and he who keeps My deeds until the end, to him I will give authority over the nations [Revelation 2:26].*

For **overcomes**, see page 35. **And he who keeps My deeds** is in contrast to "her deed," the deeds of Jezebel in verse 22.

> ▶ *And he shall rule them with a rod of iron. As the vessels of the potter are broken to pieces, as I also have received authority from My Father [Revelation 2:27].*

Verses 26 and 27 are a quote from various Old Testament passages that predict the triumph of Christ over all the nations of the world.

> Ask of Me, and I will surely give the nations as Your *inheritance*, and the very ends of the earth as Your *possession*. You shall break them with a rod of iron, You shall shatter them like earthenware [Psalm 2:8, 9].

Rule is *poimaneo*, which means "to shepherd." *As I also* shows that Christ will share His authority with all true believers, as He did with His apostles.

> Jesus summoned His twelve disciples and *gave them authority* over unclean spirits, to cast them out, and to heal every kind of disease and every kind of sickness [Matthew 10:1].

> ▶ *[A]nd I will give him the morning star. He who has an ear, let him hear what the Spirit says to the churches [Revelation 2:28, 29].*

The morning star is Christ Himself (See Revelation 22:16). For *hear*, *the Spirit*, and *churches* see page 35.

E. The letter to Sardis – Theme of the letter: wake up and finish the work of Christ, Revelation 3:1-6.

1. The Destination - The church at Sardis.

> ▶ *To the angel in Sardis write [Revelation 3:1a].*

Sardis was an important and wealthy city located about 30 miles Southeast of Thyatira on the commercial and military trade route running east and west through the sub-province of Lydia. At one time Sardis had been the capital city of the Kingdom of Lydia. It was well past its power and influence, but was still wealthy from the wool industry, the dye industry, and jewelry trade. The city was noted for pagan worship with the magnificent Temple of Artemis and many mystery cults also known as secret religious societies. Artemis (or Diana or Cybele), was the Greek goddess of fertility that some believed could restore the dead to life.

The remains of a Christian church building have been discovered immediately adjacent to the Artemis Temple, evidently a witness to this wicked and pagan city noted for its loose living. However, the Sardisians were trying to live in the present from past splendor, which led them into moral decay. The church in Sardis continued its existence until the fourteenth century but was never considered a prominent, influential church.

2. The Commendation - none given.

3. The Rebuke - for being a spiritually dead church.

> ► *He who has the seven Spirits of God and the seven stars, says this, "I know your deeds, that you have a name that you are alive, but you are dead" [Revelation 3:1b].*

He who has denotes possession, ownership and authority.

The seven Spirits of God are described in Isaiah. 11:2-5 as (1) the Lord, (2) wisdom, (3) understanding, (4) counsel, (5) might, (6) knowledge, and (7) the fear of the Lord. Collectively these attributes can be understood to be the Holy Spirit. *The seven stars* according to Revelation 1:20 are the seven angels or messengers of the seven churches. This is probably a reference to their special human messengers or pastors.

I know is *oida*, which means to know by seeing, observing. *Your deeds* are the works that a church is performing. Christ had commended the other churches for their works of love, faithfulness, perseverance, uncompromising position and refusal to deny Him. Here, Christ has no commendation, only the rebuke: *you have a name that you are alive, but you are dead.*

Name is *onoma*, which includes character and reputation. "Name" is what others thought, but what was important was what God thought, *in the sight of God* (see Revelation 3:2).

Dead refers to spiritual deadness (see Ephesians 2:1-10) Therefore, "alive" and "dead," which usually refer to physical characteristics, are here used to describe *spiritual* characteristics. A church is either alive or dead according to *God's* perspective. We can compare the reputation God requires of spiritual leaders in Paul's letters to Timothy and Titus.

An overseer, then, must be above reproach, the husband of one wife, temperate, prudent, respectable, hospitable, able to teach .... and he *must have a good reputation* with those outside the church, so that he will not fall into reproach and the snare of the devil [1 Timothy 3:2,7].

Likewise urge the young men to be sensible; in all things show yourself to *be an example* of good deeds, with purity in doctrine, dignified [Titus 1:6, 7].

Christ looks at heart motives:

But I have this against you, that you have left your first love .... I know your deeds, and your love and faith and service and perseverance, and that your deeds of late are greater than at first [Revelation 2:4, 19].

As a whole, the church at Sardis was spiritually dead, indicating that most of them were either unbelievers or believers who were out of fellowship with God, which means they were living outside the power of the indwelling Holy Spirit.

Let no one say when he is tempted, "I am being tempted by God;" for God cannot be tempted by evil, and He Himself does not tempt anyone. But each one is tempted when he is carried away and enticed by his own lust. Then when lust has conceived, it gives birth to sin; and when sin is accomplished, it brings forth death [James 1:13-15].

4. The Exhortation - to wake up and finish the work of Christ.

▶ *Wake up, and strengthen the things that remain, which were about to die; for I have not found your deeds completed in the sight of My God [Revelation 3:2].*

Wake up is a present imperative. present tense is, "stay on the alert." Imperative mood is a command. The verb is *gregoreo*, from which English derives the name "Gregory," a person who is awake and alert.

Historically, Sardis was a fortified city, protected on three sides by steep cliffs. Because of the Sardisian overconfidence in their security the city was conquered twice, first by Cyrus the Persian in 549 B.C., and again by Antiochus the Greek in 214 B.C. On both occasions the watchmen had gone to sleep at their posts.

Strengthen is also present imperative. *About to die* suggests that without the strengthening, *the things that remain* (all that Christ wants this Church to accomplish) will indeed die. Also, they can neither do the work of God nor can they "strengthen" what remains if they are themselves spiritually dead. The unbelievers in Sardis needed to trust in Christ; the believers out of fellowship needed to confess their sins.

> If we *confess our sins*, He is faithful and righteous to forgive us our sins and to cleanse us from all unrighteousness [1 John 1:9].

> ▶ *So remember what you have received and heard; and keep it, and repent. Therefore if you do not wake up, I will come like a thief, and you will not know at what hour I will come to you [Revelation 3:3].*

Remember, keep, and *repent* are all imperative commands. *What you have received and heard* has been the Gospel of Jesus Christ, which the apostles spread all over Asia Minor.

If is a Class III conditional sentence; "maybe you will and maybe you won't." The choice is up to them; no one can force someone else to trust Christ as Savior. A *thief* comes suddenly, unexpectedly, and irrevocably. A thief comes and takes something away. In this case Christ will remove their lamp, their testimony, at least what is left of it (see Revelation 2:5). *Keep* is *tareo*, which means to strictly follow. *You* is singular, referring collectively to the entire Church. For *repent*, see page 33.

5. The Promise - to fellowship with all believers and declare their name in heaven someday.

> ▶ *But you have a few people in Sardis who have not soiled their garments; and they will walk with Me in white, for they are worthy [Revelation 3:4].*

A few people are the believing remnant in the Church at Sardis. *Soiled their garments,* then, is a reference to believers in the Church who had gone the way of the world, were out of fellowship with the Lord, and were unusable to Him. In Sardis was a social register, and anyone who appeared in public with a soiled woolen garment was dropped from the register. This analogy *does not mean* that Christians *lose their salvation,* rather these were no longer available to be used of Christ to finish His works in the Church (see footnote 9, pages 56-58).

White garments in verses 4 and 5 is *leukois.* This is a different word from the "white linen" in Revelation 19:8. Likewise the word *garment* in Jude 23 is a different word, *chitona.* Verse 4, then, seems to refer to the Christian's walk or lifestyle (Greek, *peripateo)* in this life, and they become *worthy* to finish their deeds for Christ.

> ▶ *He who overcomes will thus be clothed with white garments; and I will not erase his name from the book of life, and I will confess his name before My Father and before His angels [Revelation 3:5].*

For *overcomes,* see page 35. Therefore, this verse looks further ahead to the believer in heaven. *I will not erase his name from the book of life* does not suggest that Christ ever does that. It is simply an affirmative promise of Christ that He *will not.* Since an "overcomer" is a believer ...

> For *whatever is born of God* overcomes the world; and this is the victory that has overcome the world – our faith [1 John 5:4,5].

... and a believer is *secure* in Christ ...

And the testimony is this, that God gives us eternal life, and this life is in His Son. He who has the Son has life; he who does not have the Son of God does not have the life. These things I have written to you who believe in the name of the Son of God, so that you may *know that you have eternal life* [1 John 5:11-13].

... we must not interpret this verse to suggest insecurity for the believer.[9] Since *life* here refers to *eternal life* (see John 10:27-38), the

---

[9] The Bible teaches security of the believer. Many passages verify this fact.

My sheep hear my voice, and I know them, and they follow Me; and I give eternal life to them, and they will never perish; and *no one will snatch them out* of My hand. My Father, who has given them to Me, is greater than all; and *no one is able to snatch them out* of the Father's hand. I and the Father are one [John 10:27-30].

For I am convinced that neither death, nor life, nor angels, nor principalities, nor things present, nor things to come, nor powers, nor height, nor depth, nor any other created thing, *will be able to separate us* from the love of God, which is in Christ Jesus our Lord [Romans 8:38, 39].

Now He who establishes us with you in Christ and anointed us is God, who also *sealed* us and gave us the Spirit in our hearts as a pledge [2 Corinthians 1:21, 22].

In Him, you also, after listening to the message of truth, the gospel of your salvation – having also believed, you were *sealed* in Him with the Holy Spirit of promise, who is given as a pledge of our inheritance, with a view to the redemption of God's own possession, to the praise of His glory [Ephesians 1:13, 14].

Do not grieve the Holy Spirit of God, by whom you were *sealed* for the day of redemption [Ephesians 4:30].

Blessed be the God and Father of our Lord Jesus Christ, who according to His great mercy has caused us to be born again to a living hope through the resurrection of Jesus Christ from the dead, to obtain an inheritance which is imperishable and undefiled and *will not fade away*, reserved in heaven for you, who are protected by the power of God through faith for a salvation ready to be revealed in the last time [1 Peter 1:3-5].

Since the Bible teaches this assurance of salvation, the believer can feel and know that they are saved and on their way to heaven. This assurance is a ministry of the Holy Spirit through two basic ways:

(1) By taking God at His word.

> Truly, truly I say to you, he who hears My word, and believes Him that sent Me, has *eternal* life, and does not come into judgment, but *has passed* out of death into life [John 5:24].

(2) By examining the noticeable, scriptural, spiritual life of the believer. Salvation – trusting in Jesus Christ as one's personal Savior – always must occur first. Then and only then is a person capable of producing works that God would consider as "good." The indwelling Holy Spirit assists the believer in doing "good works." This "fruit" is described in John's first epistle.

(a) Obedience to God's commandments.

> By this we know that we have come to know Him, if we *keep* His commandments [1 John 2:3].

> The one who *keeps* His commandments abides in Him, and He in him. We know by this that He abides in us, by the Spirit whom He has given us [1 John 3:24].

> For this is the love of God, that we *keep* His commandments, and His commandments are not burdensome [1 John 5:3].

(b) Practicing righteousness.

> If you know that he is righteous, you know that everyone also who *practices righteousness* is born of Him [1 John 2:29].

(c) Not practicing sinning.

> No one who is born of God *practices* sin, because his seed abides in him; and he cannot sin, because he is born of God [1 John 3:9].

> We know that no one who is born of God sins; but He who was born of God keeps him, and the evil one does not touch him [1 John 5:18].

(d) Love for other believers.

author does not agree with the interpretation that this *book of life* is all those who are physically alive, that when a person lives their whole life without accepting Christ, that when they physically die, Jesus erases their name from the book of life. Someone who had trusted Christ *has eternal life* and would *never* have their name erased (see also Revelation 20:11-15, especially verse 15).

> And if anyone's name was not found written in the book of life, he was thrown into the lake of fire [Revelation 20:15].

For *confess his name before My Father*,

> Therefore everyone who confesses me before men, I will also *confess him before My Father* who is in heaven. But whoever denies Me before men, I will also

We know that we have passed out of death into life, because we *love the brethren*. He who does not love abides in death [1 John 3:14].

This is His commandment, that we believe in the name of His Son Jesus Christ, and *love one another*, just as He has commanded us [1 John 3:24].

Beloved, let us *love one another*, for love is from God; and everyone who loves is born of God and knows God [1 John 4:7].

Whoever believes that Jesus is the Christ is born of God, and whoever loves the Father loves the child born of Him. By this we know that *we love the children of God*, when we love God and observe His commandments [1 John 5:1, 2].

The Bible teaches that the believer can operate from the old sin nature that we call "carnality." But this must never become a way of life for the believer. In Scripture, carnal believers are always chastised for being so, and exhorted to confess and forsake their sin and to walk in fellowship with God. An Old Testament example of this is found in the life of David in 2nd Samuel, chapters 11 and 12, where King David lived a life of carnality for more than a year and was severely chastised for it. David's confession of sin and renewal of his fellowship with God is found in Psalms 32, 38, and 51.

deny him before the Father who is in heaven [Matthew 10:32, 33].

The Pharisees *denied who* Jesus is.

But when the Pharisees heard this, they said, *"this man casts out demons only by Beelzebul the ruler of the demons"* [Matthew 12:24].

Peter *confessed who* Jesus is.

Simon Peter answered, *"You are the Christ, the Son of the living God"* [Matthew 16:16].

Then, in Matthew 26:75, Peter simply *denied that he knew* Christ.

And Peter remembered the word which Jesus had said, "before a rooster crows, you will *deny Me three times."* And he went out and wept bitterly [Matthew 26:75].

He was *not denying who Christ was* in the sense of Matthew 10:32-33, and certainly did not "lose" his salvation.[10]

▶ *He who has an ear, let him hear what the Spirit says to the churches [Revelation 3:6].*

See page 35.

F. The letter to Philadelphia – Theme of the letter: hold fast until Jesus returns [Revelation 3:7-13].

1. The Destination - the church at Philadelphia.

▶ *And to the angel in the church in Philadelphia write [Revelation 3:7a].*

---

[10] On security of the believer, see Steven Waterhouse, *Blessed Assurance, A Defense of the Doctrine of Eternal Security,* (Amarillo TX: Westcliff Press, 2004).

For *angel* and *church* and *write* see pages 29, 31.

Philadelphia means "brotherly love," and this was the city of brotherly love. It was located some 28 miles south of Sardis in the sub-province of Lydia. Philadelphia had a long history, but several times was almost completely destroyed by earthquakes. The most recent rebuilding before this letter had been A.D. 17.

The land around the city was rich in agriculture with grapes as one of the principal crops. Dionysus, the god of wine, was therefore one of the chief objects of pagan worship. While this letter was primarily one of praise, history tells us their Christian testimony became nominal at times, but did persevere until after World War I.

2. The Commendation - for being faithful to Christ and to the Word of God.

> ▶ ... *He who is holy, who is true, who has the key of David, who opens and no one will shut, and shuts and no one opens, says this [Revelation 3:7b].*

Holy is *hagios*, which means set apart, that which is separate from common condition and use. Christ is "set apart" from His creation; He is before it, above it, and separate from it, in purity and essence. God is in His creation by His omnipresence, but He forever remains undefiled by it.

True is *alatheia*, which means worthy of credit, truth, sincerity, veracity, and absolute truth. Christ is the source of truth and the every essence of truth.

> Jesus said to him, "I am the way, and the truth, and the life; no one comes to the Father but through Me" [John 14:6].

Notice the close ties between holiness and truth, between behavior and character, between practice and essence, between life and doctrine.

A *key* symbolizes authority and access. In Revelation 1:18, Christ has the "keys of hell and death," but here, *the key of David*. This is probably a reference to Isaiah. 22:22 where Eliakim, a type of Christ, had "the key of the house of David," which was not a reference to salvation but to opportunity, service, and testimony. The heathen culture of Philadelphia could not overrule the sovereignty of Christ in providing for these Christians an opportunity to witness for Him and to serve Him.

> *I know your deeds. Behold, I have put before you an open door which no one can shut, because you have a little power, and have kept My word, and have not denied My name [Revelation 3:8].*

For *I know your deeds* see page 31. In the light of verse 7b, *I have put before you* probably refers to their opportunity, which Christ has made available to them.

An open door may refer to the physical location of Philadelphia. Smyrna was a seaport city on the west of Lydia. A long valley stretched eastward, rising to Philadelphia. The road through the valley and through Philadelphia rose to the Great Central Plateau of Asia Minor, making Philadelphia the keeper of the gateway to the plateau and to the East. Christ calls this "an open door" without the definite article because Ephesus also had an Asian trade route with the East. If certain Christians do not take advantage of their opportunities, God will use someone else.

You have a little power is not a rebuke because of the rest of this verse. They *have kept My word and have not denied My name* in spite of their "little power," which is actually part of their commendation.

My word is the doctrine of the Apostles that had spread to the churches. Many at Thyatira had compromised their doctrine, but none of the believers at Philadelphia had compromised. *Name* is "onoma," see page 52. They had not denied Christ or anything He stands for.

Therefore everyone who confesses Me before men, I will also confess him before My Father who is in heaven. But whoever denies Me before men, him I will also deny him before My Father who is in heaven [Matthew 10:32,33].

Simon Peter answered, "You are the Christ, the Son of the living God" [Matthew 16:16].

And Peter remembered the word which Jesus said, "before a rooster crows, you will deny Me three times." And he went out and wept bitterly [Matthew 26:75].

Peter had denied that he *knew* Christ, but he never denied *who Jesus was*.[11]

3. The Rebuke - none given.

4. The Exhortation - to hold fast until Jesus returns.

> ▶ *Behold, I will cause those of the synagogue of Satan, who say that they are Jews and are not, but lie – I will make them come and bow down at your feet, and make them know that I have loved you [Revelation 3:9].*

I will cause puts the fulfillment of this verse at the Second Advent of Christ when he sets up His millennial reign, giving His followers "authority over the nations" (see Revelation 2:26), and will *make them come and bow down at your feet.*

The synagogue of Satan (see also Revelation 2:9, pp. 37-38) was Christ's description of the Jews in Philadelphia who had rejected the Christian witness and the Gospel of Christ. *Jews* in these letters, from God's perspective, then, are spiritually unfulfilled Jews who have not trusted in Christ as their Savior. John's gospel describes Jesus' description of the Christ-rejecting Jews as "of their father the devil."

> You are *of your father the devil*, and you want to do the desires of your father. He was a murderer from the beginning, and does not stand in the truth because there is no truth in him. Whenever he speaks a lie, he speaks

---

[11] For a clear interpretation of Romans 10:9 and 10, specifically, "confess Jesus before men to be saved," and an exposition of Matthew 10:32, 33 and Luke 12:8 on "denial before men," see Steven Waterhouse, *Not By Bread Alone*, 4th Ed., (Amarillo TX: Westcliff Press, 2010) p. 151ff.

from his own nature, for he is a liar and the father of lies [John 8:44].

I have loved you is from *agapao*, which means to love unconditionally, to love by choice. It is aorist tense that denotes completed action.

But God demonstrates *His own love toward us*, in that while we were yet sinners, Christ died for us [Romans 5:8].

▶ *Because you have kept the word of My perseverance, I also will keep you from the hour of testing, that hour which is about to come upon the whole world, to test those who dwell on the earth [Revelation 3:10].*

My perseverance probably refers to Christ's own endurance against sinners.

For consider Him who has *endured* such hostility by sinners against Himself, so that you will not grow weary and lose heart [Hebrews 12:3].

Thus Christ becomes the *standard* of our endurance.

The rest of this verse has been controversial for many scholars. It is vague enough to be difficult to identify *from the hour of testing* and *those who dwell on the earth*. The author believes that this verse of prophecy, like so many other such verses, has a dual fulfillment:

From is the Greek particle *ek* meaning *out of* but can be translated *from*. In John 17:15 and James 1:27 it is used with this same verb *keep* and means (1) *through*.

I do not ask You to take them *out of* the world, but to *keep them* from the evil one [John 17:15].

Pure and undefiled religion in the sight of our God and Father is this; to visit orphans and widows in their distress, and to *keep* oneself unstained by the world [James 1:27].

However, in Acts 7:10 "from" is used in an absolute sense showing that Joseph was (2) *taken away from*, out of, all his trials in prison and was never to return to them.

> [A]nd *rescued him from* all his afflictions, and granted
> him favor and wisdom in the sight of Pharaoh, King of
> Egypt, and he made him governor over Egypt and all
> his household [Acts 7:10].

Therefore, a long-range prophecy could make this verse refer to the tribulation period described in Revelation Chapters 6-18, and this verse is a promise to the church that He will rapture them *out of the world* before that Tribulation begins. Some take this simply as a promise to be with us through the trials, but that interpretation is problematic because Chapter six describes the death of many believers during the Tribulation. As a short-range prophecy, *the hour of testing* could refer to the next Roman Empire-wide persecution of Christians that came in A.D. 98 under Emperor Trajan.

The whole world, then, refers in this sense to the whole known world at that time which was the Roman Empire. *Those* in a short-term sense would refer to believers, and *those* in a long-range sense would refer to unbelievers.

> ▶ *I am coming quickly; hold fast what you have, so*
> *that no one will take your crown [Revelation 3:11].*

Quickly can have the sense of "soon," denoting a personal visit from Christ as in Revelation 2:5, 2:16, and 3:3; or it can have the sense of when Christ does come at the Rapture: it will be sudden.

Hold fast, or "keep holding fast," is done by faith. Christ does not expect us to hold fast in our own strength.

> [F]or *we walk by faith*, not by sight [2 Corinthians 5:7].

Crown is *stephanos*, which was an earned crown; see page 39.

5. The Promise - to honor every believer in the New Jerusalem.

> ▶ *He who overcomes, I will make him a pillar in the temple of My God, and he will not go out from it anymore; and I will write on him the name of My God, and the name of the city of My God, the new Jerusalem, which comes down out of heaven from My God, and My new name [Revelation 3:12].*

For **overcomes** see page 35. Whenever a new temple was built or added onto in Philadelphia, special pillars were dedicated in honor of magistrates or priests with their name engraved upon the pillar. Jesus promises such pillars for His followers **in the temple of My God. He will not go out from it anymore** describes eternal life in heaven. Three **names** will be engraved on them (probably upon their "white garments," see Revelation 2:5): the name of God, of the New Jerusalem, and the new name of Christ (see Revelation 19:12).

> ▶ *He who has an ear let him hear what the Spirit says to the churches [Revelation 3:13].*

See page 35.

G. The Letter to Laodicea – Theme of the letter: be zealous for Jesus Christ, Revelation 3:14-22.

1. The Destination - the Church at Laodicea.

> ▶ *To the angel of the church in Laodicea write...* *[Revelation 3:14a].*

For **angel** and **church** and **write** see pages 29, 31.

Laodicea was located about 40 miles southeast of Philadelphia and about 90 miles due east of Ephesus. The seven churches formed a rough circle; starting with Ephesus, the letters went clockwise from the southwest part of the circle. Under Roman rule Laodicea had become a wealthy city, mostly from the production of wool cloth. The merchants were famous for growing their own glossy black wool and making a garment that became widely sold.

The city was also famous for two kinds of medicine, namely, an ointment for sore ears and an eye powder (called "phyregian powder") for sore eyes. Their medical school at the Temple of Asclepius, the god of healing, was famous for the preparation and administration of this ointment and powder. The city was so wealthy that after an earthquake destroyed it in A.D. 60, the people refused help from Rome and rebuilt the city by themselves. Their water supply came from hot springs through a six-mile-long aqueduct from the south that cooled the water to lukewarm by the time it reached Laodicea.

Paul's references to the Laodicean church in Colossians 4:4 and 4:15-17 indicate that the Church there had been well established by A.D. 61. However, with their economic sufficiency, the Laodiceans had lulled themselves to sleep spiritually. Evidently, they repented as a result of this letter, because the church survived until the 14th century. The populace also worshipped Zeus, the chief god of the Greeks.

2.   The Commendation - none given.

3.   The Rebuke - for being lukewarm.

> ▶ *The Amen, the faithful and true Witness, the beginning of the creation of God, says this [Revelation 3:14b].*

Amen is the transliterated Greek word "amen" which means *so be it*, or "that which is sure and valid" (see also page 20).

> For as many as are the promises of God, in Him they are yes, therefore also through Him is our *Amen* to the glory of God through us [2 Corinthians 1:20].

For *faithful witness* see pages 16-17. For *true* see page 60.

Beginning is *archa*, which means *source* or *origin* (see Colossians 1:15-18). Revelation 3:14b in no way suggests Christ was created; it says that He *is* the Creator.

> He is the image of the invisible God, the firstborn of all creation. For *by Him all things were created*, both in

the heavens and on earth, visible and invisible, whether thrones or dominions or rulers or authorities – all things have been *created by Him*. He is before all things, and in Him all things hold together. He is also the head of the body, the church; and He is the beginning, the firstborn from the dead, so that He Himself will come to have first place in everything [Colossians 1:15-18].

See page 26 (Revelation 1:17) for "first and last."

Note that the Sardis (Revelation 3:1), and Laodicean churches were not good witnesses. The Philadelphian church was (Revelation 3:8).

> ► *I know your deeds, that you are neither cold nor hot; I wish that you were cold or hot [Revelation 3:15].*

For *I know* see page 31. The same word is found in verse 17; the Laodiceans *did not know* their poor spiritual condition. *You are neither cold nor hot* is perhaps also suggested in Colossians 4:15-17. If water is either "cold *or* hot" it can be refreshing, but these folk were like the lukewarm water that arrived in Laodicea. Notice that it was their *deeds* that were neither cold *nor* hot, and refers, therefore, to their lack of usefulness to Christ. *Cold,* then, does *not refer to their salvation,* because God wants all people to come to repentance.

> The Lord is not slow about His promise, as some count slowness, but is patient toward you, not wishing for any to perish but for all to *come to repentance* [2 Peter 3:9].

> ► *So because you are lukewarm, and neither hot nor cold, I will spit you out of My mouth [Revelation 3:16].*

Lukewarm is *chliaros,* which means *tepid.* It seems to be a final state of these Christians; they are neither on their way to cold nor hot, but are stuck on lukewarm. This makes it impossible for humans to determine from the deeds of a lukewarm person whether they are truly Christians or not; such lukewarmness, then, is intolerable to Christ and He will "spit them out of His mouth."

I will spit is actually *mello emesia*, which is *I am about to vomit.*

> ► *Because you say, "I am rich, and have become wealthy, and have need of nothing," and you do not know that you are wretched and miserable and poor and blind and naked [Revelation 3:17].*

Because you say is at the heart of the problem. Their view, like the Sardisians, (Revelation 3:1), was a very fleshly viewpoint. Their material richness and wealth had blinded them to their spiritual poverty.

Rich is an adjective and *have become wealthy* is the verb, but both words are from the same root. *Have become wealthy* is a perfect tense, past action with present, ongoing results; they assumed they would remain materially wealthy.

Wretched means to be plundered by war (they were spiritually plundered by their own attitude toward material wealth). *Miserable* means "pitiable." *Poor* is the word for "begging poor." *Blind* is a Scriptural term for spiritual blindness.

> And Jesus said, "For judgment I came into this world, so that those who do not see may see, and that those who see may become *blind*." Those of the Pharisees who were with Him heard these things and said to him, "We are not *blind* too, are we?" Jesus said to them, "If you were *blind*, you would have no sin; but since you say, 'we see,' your sin remains" [John 9:39-41].

Naked is used in Scripture for sin.

> Jerusalem sinned greatly, therefore she has become an unclean thing. All who honor her despise her because they have seen her *nakedness*; even she groans and turns away. Her uncleanness was in her skirts; she did not consider her future. Therefore she has fallen astonishingly; she has no comforter ... [Lamentations 1:8,9].

Notice how the material wealth of Laodicea had crept into the Church.

4. The Exhortation - Repent and be zealous for good works.

> ► *I advise you to buy from Me gold refined by fire so that you may become rich, and white garments so that you may clothe yourself, and that the shame of your nakedness will not be revealed; and eye salve to anoint your eyes so that you may see [Revelation 3:18].*

Buy from Me gold probably refers to the fruit of the Holy Spirit ...

> But the *fruit of the Spirit* is love, joy, peace, patience, kindness, goodness, faithfulness, gentleness, self-control, against such things there is no law [Gal. 5:22,23].

... which Paul describes as "gold, silver, and precious stones."

> Now if any man builds on the foundation with *gold, silver, precious stones*, wood, hay, straw, each man's work will become evident, for the day will show it because it is to be revealed by fire, and the fire itself will test the quality of each man's work. If any man's work which he has built on it remains, he will receive a reward. If any man's work is burned up, he will suffer loss; but he himself will be saved, yet so as through fire [1 Corinthians 3:12-15].

White garments is *himatia leuka,* which are those that are "not soiled" as they were in Sardis (Revelation 3:4). ***Eye salve*** was a reference to the eye salve that was manufactured in Laodicea.

> ► *Those whom I love, I reprove and discipline; therefore be zealous and repent [Revelation 3:19].*

I love is *phileo,* which means affectionate love, the love for a brother. ***Reprove*** is *elegcho,* meaning to expose, convict, punish (usually verbally, but not always). ***Discipline*** is *paideuo,* which means to train, discipline, and educate a child. Christ would not "reprove or discipline" an unbeliever, only a believer. ***Be zealous*** is *zaleuo,* to be hot, to have strong affection toward.

[I]n all things show yourself to be an example of good deeds, with purity in doctrine, dignified .... who gave Himself for us to redeem us from every lawless deed, and to purify for Himself a people for His own possession, *zealous* for good deeds .... remind them to be subject to rulers , to authorities, to be obedient, to be ready for every good deed .... For we are His workmanship, created in Christ Jesus for good works, which God prepared beforehand so that we should walk in them [Titus 2:7, 14; 3:1; Ephesians 2:10].

For **Repent** see page 33.

5. The Promise - of sweet fellowship now, and shared rule in, the millennial reign of Christ.

▶ *Behold I stand at the door and knock; if anyone hears My voice and opens the door, I will come in to him and will dine with him, and he with Me [Revelation 3:20].*

This verse has often been used in evangelism, but the context is dealing with believers who are out of fellowship with Christ.

I am the vine, you are the branches; he who abides in Me and I in him, he bears much fruit, for *apart from Me* you can do nothing [John 15:5].

The door may refer to the door of the Church building, or perhaps the door of a person's heart, the verse just does not say. **Anyone, him,** and **he** are all singular, which teaches two things: (1) that fellowship with Christ is an individual thing between Christ and the person; the Church as a whole assembly cannot give a person fellowship with Christ, and (2) individuals can have fellowship with Christ even if most of the Church is out of fellowship as at Sardis.

Come in to him, and will dine with him speaks of fellowship, not salvation. **Will dine** is *deipneo*, which was the main meal of the day and was the time for friends and honored guests.

In to is *pros*, which normally means "toward or up to." The word *eis*, which normally means *into* as coming into a person's body, is used eight times in the New Testament. All eight are found in the Gospel accounts and all eight describe a demon coming into a person's body (with no personal relationship with that person).

> ▶ *He who overcomes, I will grant to him to sit down with Me on My throne, as I also overcame and sat down with My Father on His throne [Revelation 3:21].*

For *overcomes* see page 35.

Grant is from *didomi*, "to give freely" (see Ephesians 2:8-9). *Gift*, therefore, means that this right to rule with Christ is something granted, not earned.

My throne is different from *His throne*, that is, the Father's throne in heaven. The *throne of Christ* is the earthly millennial throne of David.

> But when the Son of Man comes in His glory, and all the angels with Him, then He will sit on His glorious *throne* [Matthew 25:31].

New Testament believers will also sit on thrones; the Scriptures say:

> Or do you not know that the *saints will judge* the world? If the world is judged by you, are you not competent to constitute the smallest law courts? Do you not know that *we will judge* angels? How much more matters in this life? [1 Corinthians 6:2,3].

I also overcame was by faith.

> And He went a little beyond them, and fell on His face and prayed saying, "My Father, if it is possible, let this cup pass from Me; yet not as I will, but as You will" [Matthew 26:39].

And that's how we also overcome.

71

III. FUTURE - *Write the things which shall take place.*

A. Heavenly preparation for the Great Tribulation, Chapters 4 and 5.

In Chapter 4, John moves to the third division of his inspired outline recorded in Revelation 1:19.

1. God is recognized and worshipped in heaven, Revelation 4:1-11.

The things which shall take place (see Revelation 1:19). Chapters 4-22 are all yet *unfulfilled prophecy.* In Chapter 4, the scene moves from the churches on earth to the throne room in the Third Heaven.

> I know a man in Christ who fourteen years ago –
> whether in the body, I do not know, or out of the body
> I do not know, God knows – such a man was caught up
> to the *third heaven* [2 Corinthians 12:2].

God is the focus of Chapter 4 and He is being worshipped and served in heaven. This chapter anticipates that what is commonplace in heaven will someday be accomplished universally.

a. John sees God on His throne in heaven.

> ▶ *After these things I looked, and behold, a door standing open in heaven, and the first voice which I had heard, like the sound of a trumpet speaking with me, said, "Come up here, and I will show you what must take place after these things" [Revelation 4:1].*

After these things denotes a major chronological break between Chapter 3 and Chapter 4.

I looked and behold is repeated several times in the book as John will faithfully record what he saw. He did not always understand it, but would always tell us what he saw.

A door standing open in heaven is accompanied with an invitation to *come up here.* The *first voice* he heard was in Revelation 1:10, that of the resurrected, glorified Jesus Christ. Now Christ invites John up into the Third Heaven where He is.

> Do not let your heart be troubled; believe in God, believe also in Me. In My Father's house are many dwelling places; if it were not so, I would have told you; for I go to prepare a place for you. If I go and prepare a place for you, I will come again and receive you to Myself, that where I am, there you may be also [John 14:1-3].

Some take John to be a type of the Church when Jesus raptures it away and takes it to heaven with Him (1 Thessalonians 4:13-18).[12] The invitation includes the promise to *show you what must take place after these things*. Chapters 6-18 of the Book of the Revelation are interpreted to be a description of the Tribulation; Daniel's *70th Week*, Jacob's *Time of Trouble*. Therefore, all that Christ will tell John fits with the theme of this chapter, that all of God's plan is marching mankind and heaven toward a universal worship and service to God. The Tribulation is necessary punishment before man will bow the knee to God.

> For this reason also, God highly exalted Him, and bestowed upon Him the name which is above every name, so that at the name of Jesus *every knee will bow*, of those who are in heaven and on earth and under the earth, and that every tongue will confess that Jesus Christ is Lord, to the glory of God the Father [Philippians 2:9-11].

> ▶ *Immediately I was in the Spirit; and behold, a throne was standing in heaven, and One sitting on the throne [Revelation 4:2].*

In the Spirit (see Revelation 1:10, page 22), could mean that John was transported in his spirit to the Third Heaven; he did not necessarily have to go there physically. *Throne* is *thronos*, from the verb *thrao*,

---

[12] See illustration four for the sequence of God's prophetic calendar.

Illustration Four – God's Prophetic Calendar

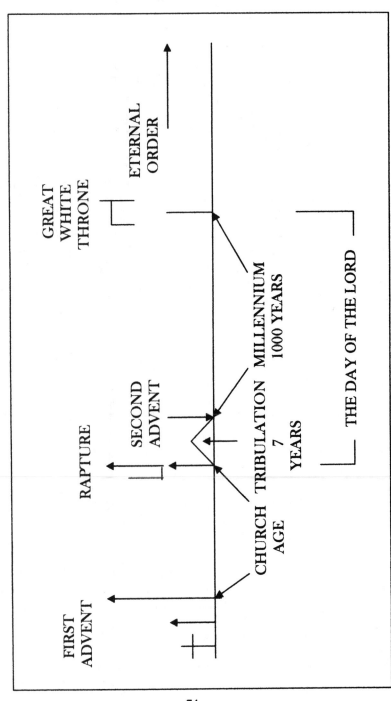

which means *to sit* (with power, authority, and dominion, see verse 11). See also Isaiah Chapters 6 and 14 and Ezekiel Chapter 1.

Standing in heaven means that it was hovering there without any visible means of support, because God's throne is not dependent upon any other source of power except Himself. ***One sitting on the throne*** is probably God the Father; this is supported by Revelation 5:5-7.

> ► *And He who was sitting was like a jasper stone and a sardius in appearance; and there was a rainbow around the throne, like an emerald in appearance [Revelation 4:3].*

Jasper stone is clear like a diamond and represents purity. The ***sardius*** is blood red and represents the redemptive blood of Jesus Christ. The ***rainbow*** symbolizes the mercy and grace of God (See Genesis 9:13-17), and God's promise of safety and salvation to all who trust in Him. This rainbow, however, was emerald, a light green in color, instead of the normal multiplicity of colors.

b. John sees the elders and living creatures.

> ► *Around the throne were twenty-four thrones; and upon the thrones I saw twenty-four elders sitting, clothed in white garments, and golden crowns on their heads [Revelation 4:4].*

The throne has the definite article; the throne of God is always the center of attention in heaven. The ***twenty-four thrones*** were ***around*** the throne. The ***twenty-four elders*** are difficult to identify. As twelve is the number of divine government in Scripture (12 tribes, 12 apostles, 12 gates in the New Jerusalem, 12 angels at each gate, 12 lunar months), the number 24 is a number of divine spiritual government. It was the number of the orders of priests in the days of David and Solomon. Here they are probably the believer priests of the Church (see Revelation 1:6), now raptured into the Third Heaven.

[A]nd He has made us to be a kingdom, priests to His God and Father – to Him be the glory and the dominion forever and ever [Revelation 1:6].

Since scholars offer 13 different explanations of whom these elders are, it is not wise to be dogmatic. *Elders* is *presbuteros*, used of the Church leaders.

> For this reason I left you in Crete, that you would set in order what remains and appoint *elders* in every city as I directed you [Titus 1:5].

> Therefore I exhort the *elders* among you, as your fellow *elder* and witness of the sufferings of Christ, and a partaker also of the glory that is to be revealed [1 Peter 5:1].

It is also used of the Jewish elders in the Gospels.

> From that time Jesus began to show His disciples that He must go to Jerusalem, and suffer many things from the *elders* and chief priests and scribes ... [Matthew 16:21a].

> When they had been released, they went to their own companions and reported all that the chief priests and *elders* had said to them [Acts 4:23].

White garments is *himatiois* and *leukios*, which evidently refer to deeds of members of the churches on earth (see also Revelation 3:4, 18). The *crowns* also are earned; *stephanos* means an earned crown that the church members would receive as rewards (cf. Revelation 2:10, 3:11. 3:18). Rewards come at the *Bema Seat*, one of ten judgments in Holy Scripture.[13]

What John was seeing then, was probably the raptured, rewarded, Church, serving God in Heaven before the record of the Tribulation begins in Chapter 6.

---

[13] See illustration five.

Illustration Five – The Ten Judgments in Scripture

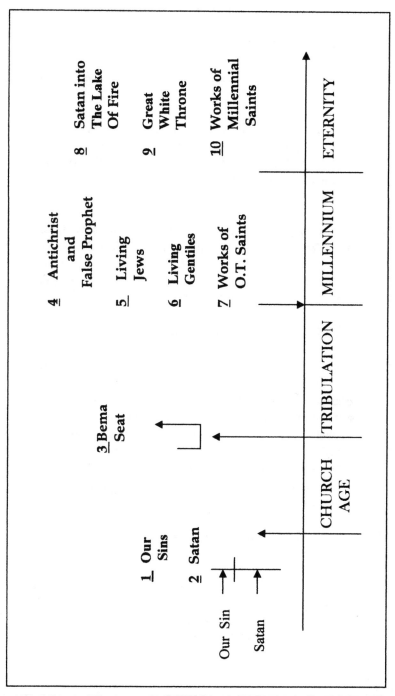

▶ *Out from the throne come flashes of lightning and sounds and peals of thunder. And there were seven lamps of fire burning before the throne, which are the seven Spirits of God [Revelation 4:5].*

Lightning and sounds and peals of thunder often accompanied divine proclamation.

So it came about on the third day, when it was morning, that there were *thunder and lightning flashes* and a thick cloud upon the mountain and a very loud trumpet sound, so that all the people who were in the camp trembled [Exodus 19:16].

Seven lamps of fire are like the "dove" of Matthew 3:16, and the "tongues of fire" of Acts 2:1-4 that enabled the Holy Spirit to be seen.

After being baptized, Jesus came up immediately from the water; and behold, the heavens were opened, and He saw the Spirit of God descending as a *dove* and lighting on Him [Matthew 3:16].

When the day of Pentecost had come, they were all together in one place. And suddenly there came from heaven a noise like a violent rushing wind, and it filled the whole house where they were sitting. And there appeared to them *tongues as of fire* distributing themselves, and they rested on each one of them. And they were all filled with the Holy Spirit and began to speak with other tongues, as the Spirit was giving them utterance [Acts 2:1-4].

The **seven Spirits of God** is the Holy Spirit (see also Revelation 1:4, 3:1, and 4:5).

▶ *[A]nd before the throne there was something like a sea of glass, like crystal; and in the center and around the throne, four living creatures full of eyes in front and behind [Revelation 4:6].*

A *sea of glass like crystal* was probably the brazen laver before the throne (See 1 Kings 7:23-26). Glass is reflective and was undisturbed, because the "elders" had no need of washing before they served God.

> And there is *no creature hidden* from His sight, but all things are open and *laid bare* to the eyes of Him with whom we have to do [Hebrews 4:13].

The *four living creatures* were *in the center and around the throne* so God's throne was the focus and probably surrounded by these creatures. *Full of eyes* denotes the Omniscience of God, as these creatures display His exceeding knowledge.

> ► *The first creature was like a lion, and the second creature like a calf, and the third creature had a face like that of a man, and the fourth creature was like a flying eagle [Revelation 4:7].*

Lion represents kingly majesty, as Christ is portrayed in the Gospel of Matthew, the King of the Jews. *Calf* is the suffering servant and perfect sacrifice, Mark's Gospel. *Man*, the Perfect Man as portrayed by Luke; perfect intelligence and reason. *Flying eagle* is sovereignty and supremacy coming from heaven; the Son of God as portrayed by John.

c. The living creatures are worshipping God.

> ► *And the four living creatures, each one of them having six wings, are full of eyes around and within; and day and night they do not cease to say, "Holy, holy, holy is the Lord God, the Almighty, who was and is and is to come" [Revelation 4:8].*

For *six wings* see Isaiah. 6:1-3, the Seraphim angels.

> In the year of King Uzziah's death I saw the Lord sitting on a throne, lofty and exalted, with the train of His robe filling the temple. Seraphim stood above Him, each having *six wings*: with two he covered his face, and with two he covered his feet, and with two he flew. And one called out to another and said, "Holy,

Holy, Holy, is the Lord of hosts, the whole earth is full
of His glory" [Isaiah. 6:1-3].

Holy, holy, holy is a superlative ("Holy and awesome is His name,"
Psalm 111:9c). *Hagios* means separated one. *Lord God* stresses Deity.
The Almighty stresses Omnipotence. *Who was and is and is to come*
stresses eternality (see also verses 9 and 10).

> ► *And when the living creatures give glory and honor
> and thanks to Him who sits on the throne, to Him who
> lives forever and ever [Revelation 4:9].*

d. The elders are worshipping God.

The throne remains the center of attention.

> ► *[T]he twenty four elders will fall down before Him
> who sits on the throne, and will worship Him who lives
> forever and ever, and will cast their crowns before the
> throne saying [Revelation 4:10].*

Cast their crowns means they acknowledge that their rewards have
come from a gracious God. After their worship, their crowns are
retrieved, for they will reign with Christ for 1,000 years.

> ► *Worthy are You, our Lord and our God, to receive
> glory and honor and power; for You created all things,
> and because of Your will they existed, and were
> created [Revelation 4:11].*

Created is an aorist tense, completed action, stressing the start of
existence. *They existed* is imperfect tense, continuous action in past
time, stressing the fact of existence. *Were created* is aorist passive,
completed action, stressing that God alone did the creating.

2. The Book of God's Redemption is given to Jesus Christ, Revelation
5:1-14.

All unbelievers and most Christians today are occupied with the
temporal things of this present world, things that can be seen and

touched and felt, things that are perishing. Too often our thoughts and speech and behavior in life have little or nothing to do with eternal values. Chapter 5 shows the proper focus of Christian lives upon the plans of God and eternal things. When God's plans are in view, the result is one of praise and worship of God while awaiting the fulfillment of His prophetic Word.

In this second chapter of heavenly activity (Chapter 4 was the first), John sees God beginning to consummate His plans to redeem the earth. Unfortunately, these plans must include a terrible judgment upon the earth because man, at large, has rejected Jesus Christ.

> The Lord is not slow about His promise, as some count slowness, but is patient toward you, not wishing for any to perish but for all to come to repentance [2 Peter 3:9].

When those in heaven and on earth witness the beginning of God's redemption, they immediately turn to praise and worship.

> [L]ooking for and hastening the coming of the day of God, because of which the *heavens will be destroyed* by burning, and the elements will melt with intense heat [2 Peter 3:12.].

a. John saw the Book of God's Redemption.

> ▶ *I saw in the right hand of Him that sat upon the throne a book written inside and on the back, sealed up with seven seals [Revelation 5:1].*

Verse one connects this chapter with Chapter 4; it is the same scene. *The right hand* represents power and authority and sovereignty and strength. *Him* is God the Father (see Revelation 4:2-3), the Ancient of Days.

> I kept looking until thrones were set up, and the *Ancient of Days* took His seat; His vesture was like white snow and the hair of His head like pure wool.

His throne was ablaze with flames, its wheels were a burning fire [Daniel 7:9].

For *the throne* see pages 73, 75. ***Book*** is the Greek word *biblion*, which gives us the word *Bible*. The book had writing *on the back*, which contained qualifications of those to open the book; the one qualified could break the seals and read on the inside. The ***inside*** writing contained the instructions to redeem a parcel of land (see Jeremiah 32:6-15); in this case, the land promised to Israel and perhaps all the earth (see Psalm 2). A Roman will was sealed with *seven seals*.

> ► *And I saw a strong angel proclaiming with a loud voice, "Who is worthy to open the book and to break its seals?" [Revelation 5:2].*

Strong is *churos*, which means powerful and mighty. This angel might be Gabriel himself. ***Who is worthy*** denotes that the angel knows the requirements written on the book. ***Worthy*** is the Greek word *haksios*, which means deserving, of equal value, comparable, equal in rank to Him who sits on the throne, someone who is qualified as a Redeemer. All of the seven ***seals*** had to be broken as the scroll or book was unrolled.

> ► *And no one in heaven or on the earth or under the earth was able to open the book or look into it [Revelation 5:3].*

Under the earth would include all those humans who had died and were still in Sheol, waiting final judgment. ***Was able*** is another key verb. It is *edunato*, which means to have power and authority.

And Jesus came up and spoke to them, saying, "all *authority* has been given to Me in heaven and on earth" [Matthew 28:18].

He said to them, "It is not for you to know times or epochs which the Father has fixed by His own *authority*" [Acts 1:7].

> ► *Then I began to weep greatly because no one was found worthy to open the book or to look into it [Revelation 5:4].*

Weep is *klao*, which means to weep openly, to visibly weep. John began to weep because he did not know what was about to happen next.

> ► *[A]nd one of the elders said to me, "Stop weeping; behold, the Lion that is from the tribe of Judah, the Root of David, has overcome so as to open the book and its seven seals" [Revelation 5:5].*

One of the elders said shows that if the elders represent the raptured Church, that which the Apostle Paul predicted will come to pass.

> For now we see in a mirror dimly, but then face-to-face, now I know in part, but then *I will know fully* just as I also have been fully known [1 Corinthians 13:12].

Stop weeping is imperative mood, a command. *Lion* was the symbol for the tribe of Judah.

> *Judah is a lion's whelp*; from the prey, my son, you have gone up. He crouches, he lies down as a lion, and as a lion, who dares rouse him up? The scepter shall not depart from Judah, nor the ruler's staff from between his feet, until Shiloh comes, and to him shall be the obedience of the peoples [Gen: 49:9, 10].

The *Root of David* refers back to Isaiah.

> Then a shoot will spring from the stem of Jesse, and a branch from his roots will bear fruit [Isaiah. 11:1].

These titles speak of kingship, judgeship, and government.

Has overcome is *enikasen*, which means "has conquered" (see also Revelation 3:21).

b. Jesus took the Book of God's Redemption.

> ► *And I saw between the throne (with the four living creatures) and the elders a lamb standing, as if slain, having seven horns and seven eyes, which are the seven Spirits of God, sent out into all the earth [Revelation 5:6].*

Between can be translated "in the midst" or "in the center." **Lamb,** when it describes Jesus, stresses His Saviorhood and the grace of God.

> The next day he saw Jesus coming to him and said, "behold, the *Lamb of God* who takes away the sin of the world!" [John 1:29].

As if slain probably means He was covered with blood, His own blood, but He was alive, resurrected! **Horns** in Scripture denote strength, and the prerogative of a king. **The seven Spirits of God** is the Holy Spirit (see also page 73). **Sent out** was predicted in John's Gospel.

> But I tell you the truth, it is to your advantage that I go away, for if I do not go away, the Helper will not come to you; but if I go away, *I will send Him* to you [John 16:7].

> ► *And He came and took the book out of the right hand of Him that sat on the throne [Revelation 5:7].*

He came and took the book (see also Revelation 6:1), shows the great power, authority, and position of Jesus Christ.

> I kept looking in the night visions, and behold, with the clouds of heaven One like a Son of Man was coming, and He came up to the Ancient of Days and was presented before Him. And to Him *was given dominion, glory and a kingdom,* that all the peoples, nations, and men of every language might serve Him. His *dominion is an everlasting dominion* which will not pass away; and His kingdom is one which *will not be destroyed* [Daniel 7:13-14].

c. When Jesus took the Book, everyone began to praise and worship God.

(1) The four living creatures and the twenty-four elders.

> ▶ *When He had taken the book, the four living creatures and the twenty-four elders fell down before the Lamb, each one holding a harp and golden bowls full of incense, which are the prayers of the saints [Revelation 5:8].*

A harp is an instrument of worship.

> Sing unto the Lord with thanksgiving; sing praise upon the *harp* unto our God [Psalm 147:7 (KJV)].

Bowls can be translated "saucers" that had handles on them. *The saints* are *hagioi*, which means *holy ones*, set apart ones, sanctified ones, and here probably refers to all true believers of every age that are now in heaven. This includes the raptured Church.

(2) The saints.

> ▶ *And they sang a new song saying, "Worthy are You to take the book and break its seals; for You were slain, and purchased for God with Your blood men from every tribe and tongue and nation" [Revelation 5:9].*

They is a personal pronoun that identifies with the nearest previous noun, which is "saints" in verse 8. *New* is *kainos*, which means freshness, and is not new in relation to time. This song is brand new, never having been sung before; that is, because Jesus had never before claimed the Book of Redemption from God the Father. *Worthy* is the same word as in verse two. To explain why, *for* is *hoti*; because of His shed blood, Jesus has gained this authority and status. *Every tribe* refers to the Church, not Israel.

> ▶ *You have made them to be a kingdom and priests to our God; and they will reign upon the earth [Revelation 5:10].*

They will reign upon the earth suggests the saints. The Church is now in heaven and must return to the earth. For **kingdom and priests** see pages 19-21 and Revelation 20:1-6, pages 196-203.

(3) The holy angels.

> ▶ *Then I looked, and I heard the voices of many angels around the throne and the living creatures and the elders; and the number of them was myriads of myriads, and thousands of thousands [Revelation 5:11].*

Many angels are the holy angels who live in heaven and constantly serve God. **Myriads of myriads, and thousands of thousands** is hyperbole for an innumerable host. Hyperbole is a figure of speech that uses exaggeration for the sake of emphasis.

> ▶ *[S]aying with a loud voice, "Worthy is the lamb that was slain to receive power and riches and wisdom and might and honor and glory and blessing" [Revelation 5:12].*

Saying is usually what angels do instead of "singing." The only other reference in Scripture for angels "singing" is Job 38:7.

> When the morning stars *sang together* and all the sons of God shouted for joy [Job 38:7].

Sons of God is an Old Testament phrase that sometimes refers to angels.

> (T)hat the *sons of God* saw that the daughters of men were beautiful; and they took wives for themselves, whomever they chose [Genesis 6:2].

> Now there was a day when the *sons of God* came to present themselves before the Lord ... [Job 1:6a].

Slain keeps being mentioned to show that Jesus had to die for our sins before God the Father exalted Him and gave Him a name above every name.

> Being found in appearance as a man, He humbled Himself by becoming obedient to the point of death, even death on a cross. For this reason also, God highly exalted Him, and bestowed on Him the name which is above every name [Philippians 2:8, 9].

Here John records their saying which includes seven attributes of God: *power, riches, wisdom, might, honor, glory, and blessing.*

(4) Every created thing.

> ▶ *And every created thing which is in heaven and on the earth and under the earth and on the sea, and all things in them, I heard saying, "To Him who sits on the throne, and to the Lamb, be blessing and honor and glory and dominion forever and ever" [Revelation 5:13].*

To Him who sits on the throne, and to the Lamb shows that the Father and the Son are equally worshiped because they are *both* Deity.

> ▶ *And the four living creatures kept saying, "Amen." And the elders fell down and worshiped [Revelation 5:14].*

Kept saying is probably a constantive aorist, which means every time someone sang or said something, the four living creatures said *Amen*, which is Greek *amen,* meaning, "so be it." Amen was used to verify or amplify what was said. Jesus said it many times in His teaching, but would use it *twice before* His teaching. The King James Version translates *amen* "verily, verily;" the New American Standard Version, "truly, truly."

In conclusion, when our attention is concentrated upon God and His plans and purposes, then we will also praise and worship Him as those portrayed in this chapter. We will then stop being preoccupied with the temporal things of this world.

B. The Tribulation, Chapters 6-18.

1. The first three and one-half years of the Tribulation, Chapters 6 and 7.

a. The Seven Seal Judgments begin the redemption of the earth, Revelation 6:1-17.[14]

(1) The first seal releases a world dictator.

> ► *Then I saw when the Lamb broke one of seven seals, and I heard one of the four living creatures saying as with a voice of thunder, "Come" [Revelation 6:1].*

Then connects this chapter with Chapters 4 and 5, which described the heavenly scene. The order is strictly chronological; therefore, the Rapture of the Church has already occurred, beginning the Tribulation. Now the opening of the seals will begin God's judgments. **Broke** denotes a point of no return. Once the first seal is broken, the demands of the document must be carried out. In the ancient world the document was a written scroll, rolled up, with wax sealing each part closed. Each seal of wax had to be broken as the scroll was unrolled.

A voice of thunder probably applies to all four of the living creatures. "Thunder" often accompanies the announcement or commencement of God's judgment. *Come* shows God's sovereignty in holding back this judgment until He pronounces it to begin.

> ► *I looked, and behold, a white horse, and he who sat upon it had a bow; and a crown was given to him, and he went out conquering and to conquer [Revelation 6:2].*

---

[14] See illustration six for the sequence of God's judgment in the Tribulation.

Illustration Six – Daniel's 70th Week

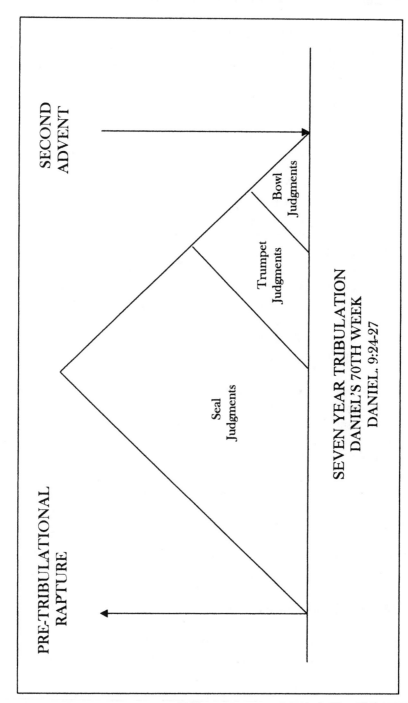

A white horse is associated by some with the Lord Jesus Christ, but a look at Revelation 19:11-13 gives a different description for Christ (see pages 190ff.). Furthermore, the subsequent events of the seals are war and death, while the subsequent events of Christ are peace and judgments. *White* describes the horse, not the rider, so it probably does not refer to Christ or to righteousness, but a pseudo-Christ with a pseudo-righteousness, the leader of a false religious system.

He, then, would refer to the antichrist, the beast of Revelation 13:1-10, which fits the "conquering," and the "prince who is to come."

> Then after the sixty-two weeks the Messiah will be cut off and have nothing, and the people of the *prince who is to come* will destroy the city and the sanctuary. And its end will come with a flood; even to the end there will be war; desolations are determined. And he will make a firm covenant with the many for one week, but in the middle of the week he will put a stop to sacrifice and grain offering; and on the wing of abominations will come one who makes desolate, even until a complete destruction, one that is decreed, is poured out on the one who makes desolate [Daniel 9:26-27].

A bow was a common Asian symbol for war, and the *crown* is *stephanos*, which was a victor's crown, an earned crown, to be distinguished from the *diadama*, or kingly crown of Revelation 19:12. The Greek word stephanos gives the English proper names "Steven" (Stephen) and "Stephanie."

Conquering and to conquer denotes a prolonged military campaign.

(2) The second seal releases world war.

> ► *When He broke the second seal, I heard the second living creature saying, "Come" [Revelation 6:3].*

The second living creature spoke in conjunction with the second seal.

> ► *And another, a red horse, went out; and to him who sat on it, it was granted to take peace from the earth,*

and that men would slay one another; and a great sword was given to him [Revelation 6:4].

To take peace from the earth means removing peace from the *whole earth*; a world-wide conflict involving every nation of the world. The **great sword** is not identified specifically but probably refers to a great ability to conquer. Some have identified this rider as the false prophet of Revelation 13:16-18, because he possesses supernatural powers.

(3) The third seal releases world famine.

► *When He broke the third seal, I heard the third living creature say, "Come." I looked, and behold, a black horse; and he who sat on it had a pair of scales in his hand [Revelation 6:5].*

Black in the Scriptures is the color for suffering.

Our skin was *black* like an oven because of the terrible famine [Lamentations 5:10 (KJV)].

A pair of scales was used to weigh out a purchase at the market place, just as it is today. The purchase is described in the next verse.

► *And I heard something like a voice in the center of the four living creatures saying, "A quart of wheat for a denarius, and three quarts of barley for a denarius, and do not damage the oil and the wine" [Revelation 6:6].*

A quart of wheat would grind down into enough flour to make one small loaf of bread; in other words, enough for about one meal for one person. A **denarius** was about a day's wages, which in John's day would purchase about eight quarts of wheat. In other words, the famine will become so great that a day's wage will purchase only enough food for one person per day with nothing left over for anything else.

Barley was normally food for animals and so three times more could be purchased for the same amount of money. **Do not damage** seems to limit the famine to early in the Tribulation, but things will grow much worse. *Oil and wine* were other daily necessities.

(4) The fourth seal releases world disease.

> ▶ *I looked, and behold, an ashen horse; and he who sat upon it had the name Death; and Hades was following with him. Authority was given to them over a fourth of the earth, to kill with sword and with famine and with pestilence and by the wild beasts of the earth [Revelation 6:8].*

Ashen was a yellowish-green, sickly color denoting pestilence and disease. These diseases are fatal, because the rider's name is *Death*. To support this interpretation, *Hades* is the Greek word for the place of the dead. So the people affected by the rider of the ashen horse are killed, as the rest of the verse clearly says. Since the Rapture is pre-tribulational, those who will die of this disease will be *unbelievers*; when *believers* are martyred in the Tribulation, they will go to heaven, according to verse 9.

This fourth horse and rider seem to combine all four horses into *sword and famine and pestilence and wild beasts* to kill *over a fourth of the earth*. Assuming the world's population is over 6 billion, this will result in the death of more than a billion people in only 3 and one-half years!

(5) The fifth seal releases the prayers of the martyrs of the Tribulation.

> ▶ *When the Lamb broke the fifth seal, I saw underneath the altar the souls of those who had been slain because of the word of God, and because of the testimony which they had maintained [Revelation 6:9].*

The altar was where the blood of Old Testament sacrifices was poured. These *souls* or people evidently had blood spilt on the earth for the cause of Christ (see Revelation 20:4), being beheaded by the antichrist.

Testimony is the Greek word *marturian*, which gives our English *martyr*, someone who holds their testimony even unto death.

> ► *[A]nd they cried out with a loud voice, saying, "How long, O Lord, holy and true, will You refrain from judging and avenging our blood on those who dwell on the earth?" [Revelation 6:10].*

Judging and avenging belongs to God ...

> Never take your own revenge, beloved, but *leave room for the wrath of God,* for it is written, "Vengeance is mine, I will repay," says the Lord [Romans 12:19].

... not to Christians (see Matthew 5:43-48).

> ► *And there was given to each of them a white robe; and they were told that they should rest for a little while longer, until the number of their fellow servants and their brethren who were to be killed even as they had been, would be completed also [Revelation 6:11].*

*A **white robe*** indicates that believers have some kind of body in heaven while they await their resurrection body. ***Robe*** is *stola,* a different word from "garments" in Revelation 3:18, which is *himatia.* A third related term, *bussinon,* is found in Revelation 19:14, which was fine linen, explained as "the righteous acts of the saints" in Revelation 19:8. This "white robe," then, is separate clothing just for tribulational saints who are killed for their faith.

Brethren who were to be killed are examples of the permissive will of God, but the word ***completed*** shows God's sovereignty in placing limits on everything that evil men do.

(6) The sixth seal releases supernatural disasters.

(a) The supernatural disasters hit.

> ► *I looked when He broke the sixth seal, and there was a great earthquake; and the sun became black as sackcloth made of hair, and the whole moon became like blood; and the stars of the sky fell to the earth, as*

> *a fig tree casts its unripe figs when shaken by a great*
> *wind [Revelation 6:12,13].*

A great earthquake is not *the* great earthquake of Revelation 16:18-20. The judgments upon the **sun, moon** and **stars** are all spoken of in Joel 2, Matthew 24, and Acts 2. In God's judgment, as He breaks this seal, He can cause the stars to fall to the earth as easily as a strong wind knocks fruit off a tree.

> ▶ *The sky was split apart like a scroll when it is rolled*
> *up, and every mountain and island were moved out of*
> *their places [Revelation 6:14].*

The sky was split apart is predicted in Isaiah's prophecy.

> And all the host of heaven will wear away, and the sky
> will be rolled up like a scroll; all their hosts will also
> wither away as a leaf withers from the vine, or as one
> withers from the fig tree [Isaiah 34:4].

(b) The unbelievers react to God's judgment.

> ▶ *Then the kings of the earth and the great men and*
> *the commanders and the rich and the strong and every*
> *slave and free man hid themselves in the caves and*
> *among the rocks of the mountains [Revelation 6:15].*

This verse describes people at every social level; just as there are unbelievers at every level, so there can be believers at every social level.

> ▶ *[A]nd they said to the mountains and to the rocks,*
> *"Fall on us and hide us from the presence of Him who*
> *sits on the throne, and from the wrath of the Lamb"*
> *[Revelation 6:16].*

Notice that men will talk to **mountains** and **rocks**, and that these men *know who is judging them!*

Wrath is *orga*, which should be compared to 1 Thessalonians 1:10.

[A]nd to wait for His Son from heaven, whom He raised from the dead, that is Jesus, who rescues us from the *wrath* to come [1 Thessalonians 1:10].

▶ *[F]or the great day of their wrath has come, and who is able to stand? [Revelation 6:17].*

The great day is the Day of the Lord (see footnote 2, page 8).

For you yourselves know full well that the *day of the Lord* will come just like a thief in the night [1 Thessalonians 5:2].

Day is not a single 24-hour day, but a long period of time. *Their,* being plural, shows that unbelievers will recognize the Deity of Jesus Christ, but will not trust in Him for the forgiveness of their sins.

b. The first "flashback;" God seals His witnesses in the midst of judgment, Revelation 7:1-17.

It is *very important* here to recognize that the chronological order of the Book of the Revelation is rather precise. However, there are entire chapters that are like "flashbacks" that fill in detail to the events that are occurring in the chapters. Chapter 7 is the first of these flashbacks, or parentheses. The other parentheses are Chapters 10-14 and 17-18. It is virtually impossible to fit these chapters into the sequence of events until one realizes that they contain the detail of what has already been introduced.

Chapter 7, then, shows the detail from the very beginning of the Tribulation, that God in the midst of judgment has been providing a witness to the Gospel of Jesus Christ. God has always provided a witness to every generation. With the Church now raptured, He returns the gospel to the Jews.

(1) God seals 144,000 Jews who fulfill the Great Commission.

▶ *After this I saw four angels standing at the four corners of the earth, holding back the four winds of the*

*earth, so that no wind would blow on the earth or on
the sea or on any tree [Revelation 7:1].*

After this I saw does not give a strict sequence of events that follow the events of Chapter 6, but simply states that this is the next thing that John saw. *Angels* is *angelos*, which means messenger, but sometimes in Scripture, especially in the Book of the Revelation, angels are used to deliver terrible judgments as described in Chapter 6.

The four corners of the earth are the four points of the compass. *Holding back the four winds* shows the tremendous power that God gives to some of His angels. *No wind would blow* would result in the cessation of weather patterns which would result in crop failure on a global scale. This probably fits, then, in the third Seal Judgment of Revelation 6:5-6.

> ► *And I saw another angel ascending from the rising
> of the sun, having the seal of the living God; and he
> cried out with a loud voice to the four angels to whom
> it was granted to harm the earth and the sea
> [Revelation 7:2].*

From the rising of the sun is the Scriptural direction of God, which is why the gate of the Tabernacle and later the Temple always faced east.

> Now those who were to camp before the tabernacle
> eastward, before the tent of meeting toward the sunrise
> … [Numbers 3:38a].[15]

Seal is the Greek word *sphragis*, which can be translated "seal" or "signet ring." Therefore, God has a seal or signet ring that He has entrusted to this angel. *To harm the earth and the sea* proves that holding back the four winds will hurt the earth and sea and is part of God's judgment.

> ► *[S]aying, "Do not harm the earth or the sea or the
> trees until we have sealed the bond-servants of our
> God on their foreheads" [Revelation 7:3].*

---

[15] Today we bury bodies with the head in the West so when they sit up at the resurrection they will be facing East.

The judgment of Revelation 6:5-6 is thus delayed until this sealing task is done, and the *we* indicates that all five angels work together in accomplishing this task.

Bond-servants is *doulos*, which in the New Testament was a willing slave or servant; these are willing, Jewish believers as the following verses will show.

On their foreheads is a very conspicuous place to put a seal. *No one* will be able to mistake who these servants are. Notice from Revelation 13:16 that the false prophet (directed by Satan himself) can only counterfeit what God has already done. Nothing is original with the Devil.

> ► *And I heard the number of those who were sealed,*
> *one hundred and forty-four thousand sealed from every*
> *tribe of the sons of Israel [Revelation 7:4].*

One hundred and forty-four thousand is a multiple of twelve; 12,000 from each of twelve tribes. Twelve is the Scriptural number for divine government and usually applied to the nation Israel. These 144,000 should be taken quite literally, because they are God's organized, missionary agency to the entire world throughout the Tribulation. God will continue to witness to the world as He judges it. **From every tribe** means there are twelve tribes, but some changes have been made; the tribe of Dan is missing, probably for the sin of idolatry (see also Judges 18).

> The son of the Israelite woman *blasphemed* the Name and cursed ... (now his mother's name was Shelomith, the daughter of Dibri, of the *tribe of Dan*) [Leviticus 24:11].

> So the king consulted, and made two golden calves, and he said to them, "It is too much for you to go up to Jerusalem; behold your gods, O Israel, that brought you up from the land of Egypt. He set one in Bethel, and the other one *he put in Dan* [1 Kings 12:28, 29].

The tribe of Ephraim is also missing, probably for the same reason. These tribes have been replaced with the tribes of Levi and Joseph. Levi belonged to the Lord and did not receive any land. Notice also that Reuben, who was the first-born, has moved to second place and Judah (the tribe of Christ) has moved to first.

Notice something very subtle about Revelation 7. Verses 1-8 talk of a very special group of people, 144,000 Jews, 12,000 from each tribe. Verses 9-17 speak of *another* very special group of people, people from every nation and tribe from around the world. This second group is obviously Gentiles who have been saved through the preaching of the 144,000 Jews; however, because they have not been sealed and preserved, many of them are martyred for their faith.

(2) The Gentiles who are martyred in the Tribulation are serving God in heaven.

> ► *After these things I looked, and behold, a great multitude which no one could count, from every nation and all tribes and people and tongues, standing before the throne and before the Lamb, clothed in white robes, and palm branches were in their hands [Revelation 7:9].*

After these things again simply describes what John was privileged to see next in this great revelation. *A great multitude* is obviously people from the earth as the verse describes. This group is in contrast with those of Revelation 5:11, which were mostly holy angels.

Standing before the throne shows that they have moved, because we said that the group in Revelation 6:9-11 were tribulational saints who were killed for their testimony. In Revelation 6:11 they were given *white robes*; the Greek is *stola leuka*. Then, in Revelation 7:9, the group John sees is *clothed in white robes*, *stola leuka*, the exact same Greek phrase. This is not to be confused with the white garment, the *himatia* of Revelation 3:18 and the fine linen, the *bussos* of Revelation 19:8 and 14, which is the Bride of Christ, 19:7, the Church.

The *stola* was a long robe, usually worn by kings or priests or someone with some kind of rank. It is the word in the Septuagint, the Greek translation of the Old Testament, used to translate the "robe" of the priests. This seems to be a special robe worn by a very special group of people, the believers martyred in the Tribulation. *Palm branches* are a sign of victory and triumph as described in Christ's Triumphal Entry.

> Most of the crowd spread their coats in the road, and others were cutting *branches* from the trees and spreading them in the road [Matthew 21:8 (see also Leviticus 23:40)].

> ▶ *[A]nd they cry out with a loud voice, saying, "Salvation to our God who sits on the throne, and to the Lamb" [Revelation 7:10].*

Salvation to our God is a poetical way of saying salvation is attributed to God.

> ▶ *And all the angels were standing around the throne and around the elders and the four living creatures; and they fell on their faces before the throne and worshipped God [Revelation 7:11].*

Now notice that in addition to the great multitude we have three other groups around God's throne, the *angels, elders, living creatures*.

> ▶ *[S]aying, "Amen, blessing and glory and wisdom and thanksgiving and honor and power and might, be to our God forever and ever. Amen" [Revelation 7:12].*

Notice there are *seven* things ascribed to God in this blessing from all the groups. Seven is the number of perfection in the Bible (refer to page 11).

> ▶ *Then one of the elders answered, saying to me, "These who are clothed in the white robes, who are they, and where have they come from?" [Revelation 7:13].*

This question is an oriental technique of teaching, anticipating that the student will ask the teacher for the answer.

> ▶ *I said to him, "My lord, you know." And he said to me, "These are the ones who come out of the great tribulation, and they have washed their robes and made them white in the blood of the Lamb"* *[Revelation 7:14].*

John's response is a polite Oriental response to give the teacher a chance to teach. Compare *the great tribulation* to that written in Matthews's Gospel.

> For then there will be a *great tribulation*, such as has not occurred since the beginning of the world until now, nor ever will [Matthew 24:21].

For *the blood of the Lamb;*

> For as for the life of all flesh, its *blood* is identified with its life ... [Leviticus 17:14a].

> ... all things are cleansed with *blood*, and without shedding of *blood* there is no forgiveness [Hebrews 9:22b].

> Be on guard for yourselves and for all the flock, among which the Holy Spirit has made you overseers, to shepherd the church of God which He purchased with His own *blood* [Acts 20:28].

> [W]hom (Christ Jesus) God displayed publicly as a propitiation in His *blood* through faith ... [Romans 3:25a].

> Much more, then, having been justified by His *blood*, we shall be saved from the wrath of God through Him [Romans 5:9].

> In Him we have redemption through His *blood*, the forgiveness of our trespasses, according to the riches of His grace [Ephesians 1:7].

[A]nd through Him to reconcile all things to Himself, having made peace through the *blood* ... [Colossians 1:20a].

[K]nowing that you were not redeemed with perishable things like silver and gold from your futile way of life inherited from your forefathers, but with precious *blood,* as of a lamb unblemished and spotless, the *blood* of Christ [1 Peter 1:18,19].

▶ *For this reason, they are before the throne of God; and they serve Him day and night in His temple; and He who sits on the throne will spread His tabernacle over them [Revelation 7:15].*

Before the throne, serve Him day and night in His temple and **spread His tabernacle over them** are all descriptions of special blessings and position for these who give their lives for God.

The King will answer and say to them, "Truly I say to you, to the extent that you did it to one of these brothers of mine, even the least of them, you did it to Me".... then He will answer them "Truly I say to you, to the extent that you did not do it to one of the least of these, you did not do it to Me" [Matthew 25:40,45].

"These my brothers" may be the group Jesus saved during the Tribulation, or it may be the 144,000. Notice that *behavior* is what reveals the spiritual condition of the sheep or the goats in Matthew's passage.

▶ *They will hunger no longer, nor thirst anymore; nor will the sun beat down on them; nor any heat [Revelation 7:16].*

This verse describes what had happened to "these my brothers," the 144,000, or the martyrs in the Tribulation.

▶ *[F]or the Lamb in the center of the throne will be their shepherd, and will guide them to springs of the*

> *water of life; and God will wipe every tear from their*
> *eyes [Revelation 7:17].*

God will wipe away every tear. This implies that there were tears in the prayers of Revelation 6:10, but God is going to wipe them away. This is one of the verses that suggests there will be tears in heaven until all of God's judgments upon man are complete.

2. The last three and one-half years of the Tribulation, Chapters 8-18.

a. The seven trumpets greatly increase God's judgment, Chapters 8-9.

(1) The first four trumpets attack lower creation, Revelation 8:1-13.

(a) The trumpets are prepared.

> ► *When the Lamb broke the seventh seal, there was*
> *silence in heaven for about half an hour [Revelation*
> *8:1].*

The **Lamb** is still the Lord Jesus Christ, cf. Revelation 6:1. **The seventh seal** picks up where the sixth seal left off (Revelation 6:12), and continues the chronology of the judgments, so that Chapter 7 was a large parenthesis.

Silence in heaven is a dramatic pause - it draws attention to the awesome power of God. In Chapters 4-7 there were seven songs of praise. The song of Revelation 4:8 was one that never ceased - until now. There is no explanation given for why the silence is **about half an hour**.

> ► *And I saw the seven angels who stand before God,*
> *and seven trumpets were given to them [Revelation*
> *8:2].*

Who stand before God shows these are very special and powerful angels. Notice their perfect submission, awaiting orders from the sovereign God of the universe. **Trumpets** is the Greek word *salpigges*, which was the silver trumpet, parallel to Numbers 10:1-10, used for announcements, warnings, and offerings. Silver is symbolic of redemption, because through His judgments God is redeeming the earth.

> ▶ *Another angel came and stood at the altar, holding a golden censer, and much incense was given to him, so that he might add it to the prayers of all the saints on the golden altar which was before the throne [Revelation 8:3].*

There are two separate altars pictured in this scene. *The altar* (the brazen altar) is the place of judgment because brass is the symbol for judgment in the Old Testament, representing the cross of Jesus Christ. *The golden altar* is the place of intercession, which is a result of the first altar because Jesus died on the cross for sins, making intercessory prayer possible. All must come to Jesus Christ either in salvation or judgment.

> As for me, I baptize you with water for repentance, but He who is coming after me is mightier than I, and I am not fit to remove His sandals; He will baptize you with the Holy Spirit and fire [Matthew 3:11].

> "Now judgment is upon this world; now the ruler of this world will be cast out. And I, if I am lifted up from the earth, *will draw all men to Myself.*" But He was saying this to indicate the kind of death by which He was to die. The crowd then answered Him, "We have heard out of the Law that the Christ is to remain forever; and how can You say, 'The Son of Man must be lifted up'? Who is this Son of Man?" [John 12:31-34].

In verse 32, "will draw all men to Myself" means that after the cross all must come to Jesus either by faith for salvation, or come before Him in judgment. Matthew 3:11 means that Jesus will baptize believers with the Holy Spirit, but baptize unbelievers in the Lake of Fire.

The prayers of all the saints were seen back in Revelation 6:9-11 and this angel is simply adding to them.

Saints is *hagioi*, which means "set apart ones," those who are set apart as holy unto God by the blood of Christ (see Revelation 7:14).

The golden altar in the Tabernacle was right in front of the veil, or in heaven, immediately *before the throne*. God's throne on earth was the Ark of the Covenant, whose lid was called the "Mercy Seat." It was God's throne on the earth for that is where He manifested His glory.

> ▶ *And the smoke of the incense, with the prayers of the saints, went up before God out of the angel's hand [Revelation 8:4].*

The prayers of the saints went up before God and resulted in tremendous action, coming in verses 5 and following. We should never doubt that prayers of believers have an effect in heaven!

> ▶ *Then the angel took the censer and filled it with the fire of the altar, and threw it to the earth; and there followed peals of thunder and sounds and flashes of lightning and an earthquake [Revelation 8:5].*

He *filled it with the fire of the altar* because that altar is the source of judgment. He *threw it to the earth* because the earth has now come under the wrath of God. *Peals of thunder and sounds and flashes of lightning* are a common Scriptural warning of immediate judgment from God. The *earthquake* is the second one; the first one is recorded in Revelation 6:12.

> ▶ *And the seven angels that had the seven trumpets prepared themselves to sound them [Revelation 8:6].*

The seven angels .... prepared themselves shows that even angels must ready themselves to do the will of God. Believers still on earth must do likewise! Note that here the four angels prepare to destroy four things we all take for granted; the land, sea, fresh water, and the heavens.

(b) The first trumpet brings judgment on the land.

> ▶ *The first sounded, and there came hail and fire, mixed with blood, and they were thrown to the earth; and a third of the earth was burned up, and a third of the trees were burned up, and all the green grass was burned up [Revelation 8:7].*

For **Hail**,

> Now the Lord said to Moses, "Stretch out your hand toward the sky, that *hail* may fall on all the land of Egypt, on man and on beast and on every plant of the field, throughout the land of Egypt." Moses stretched out his staff toward the sky, and the Lord sent thunder and *hail*, very severe, such as had not been in all the land of Egypt since it became a nation. The *hail* struck all that was in the field through all the land of Egypt, both man and beast; the *hail* also struck every plant of the field and shattered every tree of the field [Exodus 9:22-25].

The *fire* was probably lightning. **Blood** is not explained, but might be the blood of the martyred saints. *A third of the earth* is all vegetation including trees and grass. All these are essential to support man's life.

(c) The second trumpet brings judgment on the sea.

> ▶ *The second angel sounded, and something like a great mountain burning with fire was thrown into the sea; and a third of these became blood [Revelation 8:8].*

Something like shows that John really doesn't know what this is, but tries to describe it the best he can. *A third*, which is repeated all through the sounding of these trumpets, shows a *limited* judgment from God; He is still providing man an opportunity to repent. **Became blood** either from the blood of the fish in the sea, or was part of the judgment like that upon the Nile River (see Exodus 7:14-25).

▶ *[A]nd a third of the creatures which were in the sea and had life, died; and a third of the ships were destroyed [Revelation 8:9].*

A third of the ships were destroyed will include the sailors on them. If the Seal Judgments of Chapter 6 are the unleashing of man to destroy himself, then this trumpet judgment is the first of the judgments in which God directly kills man. It foreshadows Chapter 9.

(d) The third trumpet brings judgment upon the fresh water.

▶ *The third angel sounded, and a great star fell from heaven, burning like a torch, and it fell on a third of the rivers and on the springs of waters [Revelation 8:10].*

A **star** is the Greek *astar*, which gives our English words astronomy and astrology. **Rivers and springs of waters** describes fresh water which men must drink to stay alive.

▶ *The name of the star is called Wormwood; and a third of the waters became wormwood, and many men died from the waters, because they were made bitter [Revelation 8:11].*

Wormwood is a Scriptural symbol for bitterness.

But in the end she is bitter as *wormwood*, sharp as a two-edged sword [Proverbs 5:4].

He has filled me with bitterness, he has made me drunk with *wormwood* [Lamentations 3:15].

Many men died also foreshadows Revelation 9:18 ("a third of mankind was killed ...").

(e) The fourth trumpet brings judgment on the heavens.

▶ *The fourth angel sounded, and a third of the sun and a third of the moon and a third of the stars were struck; so that a third of them would be darkened and the day would not shine for a third of it, and the night in the same way [Revelation 8:12].*

Sun ... **moon** ... and **stars** have been a revelation from God.

The *heavens* are telling of the glory of God; and their *expanse* is declaring the work of His hands [Psalm 19:1 (see also Romans 1:18-25)].

But now, God is through revealing and has begun to judge. Some commentators interpret *the day would not shine for a third of it* to mean that God will simply speed up the rotation of the earth and shorten the length of the day and night. The effects will be catastrophic.

(f) Three woes are given for the three remaining trumpets.

► *Then I looked, and I heard an eagle flying in midheaven, saying with a loud voice, "Woe, woe, woe to those who dwell on the earth, because of the remaining blasts of the trumpet of the three angels who are about to sound!" [Revelation 8:13].*

An eagle in some Greek manuscripts reads "an angel." **Those who dwell on the earth** are warned because God will directly pour out His wrath upon men (Chapter 9 describes these last three trumpets).

(2) The last three trumpets attack higher creation – man, Revelation 9:1-21.

(a) The fifth trumpet judgment *torments* Christ rejectors.

► *Then the fifth angel sounded, and I saw a star from heaven which had fallen to the earth; and the key of the bottomless pit was given to him [Revelation 9:1].*

A star in the context of the third trumpet (see Revelation 8:10-11) refers to a literal heavenly body. In this context of the fifth trumpet, however, this "star" must be referring to an intelligent being.

Note that *the key* ... *was given to him* and in verse 2 "he opened" the bottomless pit. Remember that the Seal Judgments of Chapter 6 were followed by a large parenthesis, Chapter 7, which gave added details to the Seal Judgments. The same thing occurs here, except the parenthesis is larger: Chapters 8 and 9 describe the Trumpet Judgments, and Chapters 10 through 14 are a parenthesis or "flashback" to provide more detail during the Trumpet Judgments. Therefore, *from heaven* gives us a clue to the place from which this intelligent being fell. Furthermore, *which had fallen* is perfect tense, past action with present, on-going results. This being probably fell around the first of the Trumpet Judgments, which start around the middle of the Tribulation. In this context, then, the *star* is most probably Satan himself, described in Revelation 12:7-12, and Jesus Christ gives him the *key* to the *bottomless pit*. Jesus has the keys to death and Hades (see Revelation 1:18, page 26). [16]

The bottomless pit then, is probably a part of Hades. In the Greek text it reads, "the shaft of the Abyss."

> For if God did not spare angels when they sinned, but cast them into *hell* (*tartaros*) and committed them to pits of darkness, reserved for judgment [2 Peter 2:4].

> And Jesus asked him, "What is your name?" And he said, "Legion;" for many demons had entered him. They were imploring him not to command them to go away into the *abyss* [Luke 8:30, 31].

> Then I saw an angel coming down from heaven, holding the key of the *abyss* and a great chain in his

---

[16] The Bible differentiates several places of punishment. *Hell* is a general term that refers to any place of torment. *Abyss* is a Greek term often translated "pit," or "bottomless pit." The *abyss* is a temporary place of imprisonment for some fallen angels. Satan will spend 1,000 years in the abyss; after a short release he will then be cast into the *Lake of Fire* (Gehenna), the place of eternal punishment for Satan and the fallen angels, as well as, eventually, all the unsaved following final judgment at the Great White Throne. (*Tartaros* was the Greek term used to designate the place where the most wicked spirits were sent to be punished.) *Sheol* (Hebrew) and *Hades* (Greek) is the current, temporary destination of unsaved souls (humans only) immediately after death, to remain there until their condemnation at the Great White Throne judgment and transfer to the *Lake of Fire*.

hand. And he laid hold of the dragon, the serpent of old, who is the devil and Satan, and bound him for a thousand years; and he threw him into the *abyss*, and shut it and sealed it over him, so that he would not deceive the nations any longer, until the thousand years were completed; after these things he must be released for a short time [Revelation 20:1-3].

This part of Hades (called *tartaros* by Peter) is a prison for certain demons, it is the deepest abyss of Hades. Some are imprisoned there until their final judgment, but some will be loosed during the Tribulation. These demons delight in destruction and especially in killing humans.

> ▶ *He opened the bottomless pit, and smoke went up out of the pit, like the smoke of a great furnace; and the sun and the air were darkened by the smoke of the pit [Revelation 9:2].*

He opened might be compared to 2 Thessalonians 2:6-8, which suggests that the Holy Spirit indwelling the members of the Church will be taken away at the Rapture. The restraining ministry of the Holy Spirit, working through Christians, will be removed when the believers are removed.

> And you know what restrains Him now, so that in his time he will be revealed. For the mystery of lawlessness is already at work; only he who now restrains will do so until he is *taken out of the way.* Then that lawless one will be revealed whom the Lord will slay with the breath of His mouth and bring to an end by the appearance of His coming [2 Thessalonians 2:6-8].

A similar restraint has been upon those in the "shaft of the Abyss," however, this restraint is being lifted for the Tribulation.

The *smoke* here should be taken literally. It is also a foreboding announcement of the demonic oppression that is about to come over the whole earth.

> ► *Then out of the smoke came locusts upon the earth, and power was given them, as the scorpions of the earth have power [Revelation 9:3].*

The *locusts* actually come out of the smoke that darkened the sun. Context again requires us to consider these locusts as very extraordinary creatures, probably demons from the pit that take the form of locusts that will devour the earth.

Power was given them proves these locusts will be supernatural with a high degree of intelligence and with the discernment required in verse four. Locusts were the eighth plague brought upon Egypt (see Exodus 10). Joel prophesied a plague of locusts on Israel, which he used as an analogy of the future invasion into Israel during the Day of the Lord (see footnote 2, page 8).

> What the *gnawing locust* has left, the *swarming locust* has eaten; and what the swarming locust has left, the *creeping locust* has eaten; and what the creeping locust has left, the *stripping locust* has eaten. Awake, drunkards, and weep; and wail, all you wine drinkers, on account of the sweet wine that is cut off from your mouth. For a nation has *invaded* my land, mighty and without number; its teeth are the teeth of a lion, and it has the fangs of a lioness. It has made my vine a waste and my fig tree splinters. It has stripped them bare and cast them away; their branches have become white [Joel 1:4-7].

> ► *They were told not to hurt the grass of the earth; nor any green thing, nor any tree, but only the men who do not have the seal of God on their foreheads [Revelation 9:4].*

Locusts usually attack only greenery, but these are forbidden to hurt *grass* or *any green thing* or *any tree, only the men*.

The seal of God may be the sign of the cross (given to the 144,000, see Revelation 7:3), but evidently all believers in Christ will receive this seal while Christ rejectors will not, making them the targets of torment by these locust demons.

> ► *And they were not permitted to kill anyone, but to torment for five months; and their torment was like the torment of a scorpion when it stings a man [Revelation 9:5].*

The fact that the locusts *were not permitted to kill anyone* shows God's continued absolute control over His creation, even fallen angels. *Five months* was the length of time the locusts took to devastate Israel in Joel's day. Allowing this *torment* of men for five months may seem like a cruel act of God, but the rest of the chapter reveals that repentance and salvation was the desired result.

> ► *And in those days men will seek death and will not find it; they will long to die, and death flees from them [Revelation 9:6].*

In Revelation 6:16-17 the unbelievers tried to hide from the wrath of the Lamb. Now, they long to die. Unfortunately, unbelievers think that their suffering is over at physical death. In reality, *it is only the beginning!*

> Now there was a rich man, and he habitually dressed in purple and fine linen, joyously living in splendor every day. And a poor man named Lazarus was laid at his gate, covered with sores, and longing to be fed with the crumbs which were falling from the rich man's table; besides, even the dogs were coming and licking his sores. Now the poor man died and was carried away by the angels to Abraham's bosom; and the rich man also died and was buried. In Hades he lifted up his eyes, *being in torment*, and saw Abraham far away and Lazarus in his bosom. And he cried out and said, "Father Abraham, have mercy on me, and send Lazarus so that he may dip the tip of his finger in water and cool off my tongue, for *I am in agony* in this flame." But Abraham said, "Child, remember that during your life you received your good things, and

111

likewise Lazarus bad things; but now he is being comforted here, and *you are in agony*. And besides all this, between us and you there is a great chasm fixed, so that those who wish to come over from here to you will not be able, and that none may cross over from there to us." And he said, "Then I beg you, father, that you send him to my father's house – for I have five brothers – in order that he may warn them, so that they will not also come to this place of torment." But Abraham said, "They have Moses and the Prophets, let them hear them". But he said, "No, father Abraham, but if someone goes to them from the dead, they will repent!" But he said to him, "If they do not listen to Moses and the Prophets, they will not be persuaded even if someone rises from the dead" [Luke 16: 19-31].

▶ *The appearance of the locusts was **like** horses prepared for battle; and on their heads appeared to be crowns **like** gold, and their faces were **like** the faces of men. They had hair **like** the hair of women, and their teeth were **like** the teeth of lions. They had breastplates **like** breastplates of iron; and the sound of their wings was **like** the sound of chariots, of many horses rushing to battle [Revelation 9:7-10].*

This vivid description of these locusts confirms to us that these are supernatural beings. Notice, the word *like* occurs seven times in these four verses. John was trying his best to describe what he was seeing in the best terminology he could come up with. Like the locusts of Egypt "they shall cover the surface of the land .... your houses shall be filled" (see Exodus 10:5-6), there will be no escape from these horrible invaders. Their attacks will be indefensible.

▶ *They have as king over them, the angel of the abyss; his name in Hebrew is Abaddon, and in the Greek he has the name Apollyon [Revelation 9:11].*

The angel of the abyss is a *king over them* whose name is *Abaddon* and *Apollyon*, which both mean "destroyer" or "destruction." This "king" must be Satan himself. He used to appear as "an angel of light," but now has unleashed his most terrible fury.

> No wonder, for even Satan disguises himself as an *angel of light* [2 Corinthians 11:14].

> ► *The first woe is passed; behold, two woes are still coming after these things [Revelation 9:12].*

The *two* (of the three) *woes* that are still to come are: two, Revelation 9:3-21, and three, Revelation 15:1 and following. Thus, Chapters 10-14 constitute another large parenthesis.

(b) The sixth trumpet kills Christ-rejectors.

> ► *Then the sixth angel sounded, and I heard a voice from the four horns of the golden altar which is before God [Revelation 9:13].*

Voice and *golden altar* show this to be a continuation of God's answer to prayers found in Revelation 6:9-11 and Revelation 8:3-4. *Horns* is a Scriptural symbol for strength and authority.

> ► *(O)ne saying to the sixth angel who had the trumpet, "Release the four angels who are bound at the great river Euphrates" [Revelation 9:14].*

These *four angels* are not the same four angels of Revelation 7:1, because these are *bound*. This is actually a perfect passive participle from *deo*, which would translate as "who have been bound," as if for a long period of time. The angels of Revelation 7:1 were holy angels, but these are *bound*. Only fallen angels are described in Scripture as being bound. See Revelation 20:1-3 where Satan himself is bound.

This release of the angels *at the great river Euphrates* may indicate an Eastern invasion of the Middle East by the armies of the Far East (see Revelation 16:12-16, which is the 6th Bowl Judgment). It should not be assumed, however, that the 6th Trumpet coincides with the 6th Bowl, although they may be part of the same sequence of events leading to the Battle of Armageddon.

> ► *And the four angels, who had been prepared for the hour and day and month and year, were released, so that they would kill a third of mankind [Revelation 9:15].*

Notice that the only definite article appears before the word *hour*, which indicates this is a single time in history when this event must happen. *A third of mankind* is similar to Revelation 8:7-12 but reveals again a *limited* judgment on the part of God. His mercy is *still* seen even in the midst of terrible judgment!

> ► *The number of the armies of the horsemen was two hundred million; I heard the number of them [Revelation 9:16].*

Armies is literally "bodies of soldiers," which suggests an army of foot-soldiers. *Horsemen* is the same root word as "horses" back in verse 7. Here John is evidently relating this army to the tormenting demons of verses 1-12. *Two hundred million* is literally "twice myriads of myriads," the same phrase found in Revelation 5:11 that was used to describe an innumerable host. This number should be taken as general rather than specific. These "armies" could be human, demons, or demon-possessed humans. China has boasted of being able to field an army of two hundred million.

> ► *And this is how I saw in the vision the horses and those who sat on them: the riders had breastplates the color of fire and of hyacinth and of brimstone; and the heads of the horses are like the heads of lions; and out of their mouths proceed fire and smoke and brimstone. A third of mankind was killed by these three plagues, by the fire and smoke and brimstone which proceeded out of their mouths. For the power of the horses is in their mouths and in their tails; for their tails are like serpents and have heads; and with them they do harm [Revelation 9:17-19].*

Verses 17-19, like verses 7-10, may describe modern warfare or a kind of supernatural, demonic destruction.

► *The rest of mankind, who were not killed by these plagues, did not repent of the works of their hands, so as to not worship demons, and the idols of gold and of silver and of brass and of stone and of wood, which can neither see nor hear nor walk [Revelation 9:20].*

Repent is *metanoeo*, which means to change the mind (about who Jesus is and to trust Him as personal Savior). Without repentance, their "works," described in verses 20 and 21, revealed them to be Christ-rejectors.

b. The second "flashback;" description of events during the first and second halves of the Tribulation: Chapters 10-14.

These chapters do not advance the sequence of events of the Tribulation, but simply add more detail to what is happening primarily during the last half, the last three and one-half years.

(1) The little book prepares John for more prophecy, Revelation 10:1-11.

Chapter 10 is interesting because it does not in itself add much detail to God's judgments, but rather, adds detail from God's perspective and from John's perspective as to what is happening. As Daniel was physically and mentally exhausted from the visions he received concerning the "latter days ..."

> At this point the revelation ended. As for me, Daniel, my thoughts were *greatly alarming me* and my face grew pale, but I kept the matter to myself .... Then I, Daniel, *was exhausted and sick* for days. Then I got up again and carried on the king's business; but I was astounded at the vision, and there was none to explain it .... So I was left alone and saw this great vision; yet no strength was left in me for my natural *color turned to a deathly pallor,* and I *retained no strength* [Daniel 7:28, 8:27, and 10:8].

... John would have been also, except for this chapter, which explains how he was able to continue to receive the Revelation.

(a) A "strong angel" brings the little book, the book of God's judgment.

> ► *I saw another strong angel coming down out of heaven, clothed with a cloud; and the rainbow was on his head, and his face was like the sun, and his feet like pillars of fire [Revelation 10:1].*

Another is the Greek word *allos*, meaning another of the same kind. A *strong angel* was found in Revelation 5:2 and one in Revelation 8:3, but evidently this angel is yet another angel. The word *angel* is *angelos*, which actually means "messenger."

There is considerable debate as to the identity of this "strong angel." Since the chapter does not tell us, it is not essential that we identify him. It could be Gabriel or Michael or, most probably, it is Christ Himself. In this context, Christ's ministry of delivering this message to John would allow Him to be referred to as an "angel." The description of verses 1-3 seem to indicate that only Christ could be this Personage.

Regarding the reference to *a cloud,*

> And after He had said these things, He was lifted up while they were looking on, and a *cloud* received Him out of their sight. And as they were gazing intently into the sky while He was going, behold, two men in white clothing stood beside them. They also said, "Men of Galilee, who do you stand looking into the sky? This Jesus, who has been taken up from you into heaven, will come in just the same way as you have watched Him go into heaven" [Acts 1:9-11].

> Jesus said to him, "You have said it yourself; nevertheless I tell you, hereafter you will see the Son of Man sitting at the right hand of Power, and coming on the *clouds* of heaven" [Matthew 26:64].

The rainbow, a Scriptural sign of God's mercy, is around His head (see Revelation 4:3). For *face was like the sun* and *feet like pillars of fire* (see Revelation 1:15-16, pp. 25-26). These seem to describe God, not just a holy angel. If it is Christ Himself, then this mission must be very important for Him not to delegate it to anyone, choosing to do it Himself (compare "My witnesses," Revelation 11:3).

> ▶ *(A)nd he had in his hand a little book which was open. He placed his right foot on the sea and his left on the land [Revelation 10:2].*

A little book is *biblaridion*, a derivative of *biblion*, found back in Revelation 5:1. In Chapter 5 it was the *Book of Redemption*; here in Chapter 10 it is a smaller book or scroll that may be called the *Book of God's Judgment*. This book is smaller because it is a book of warnings, and there is just not much time left for planet earth.

Which was open leads some to think this is the *book* of Chapter 5. This is a perfect passive participle that can read "having been opened." This book is a book of prophecy that Christ has opened to warn the people of earth of God's imminent judgment. This is very possibly the sealed scroll of Daniel 12:1, 4, and 9, which was ordered sealed until the last days. Here John is certainly telling of the last days.

> Now at that time Michael, the great prince who stands guard over the sons of your people, will arise. And there will be a time of distress such as never occurred since there was a nation until that time; and at that time your people, everyone who is found *written in the book*, will be rescued .... but as for you, Daniel, conceal these words and seal up *the book* until the end of time; many will go back and forth, and knowledge will increase .... He said, "Go your way, Daniel, for these words are concealed and sealed up until the end of time" [Daniel 12:1, 4, 9].

The sea and *the land* can be taken two ways. This is either a reference to "Gentiles" (see Revelation 13:1), and "Jews" (see Revelation 13:11), meaning that Jesus Christ is asserting His authority over both Gentiles and Jews (His judgments will extend to *both*), or it also could be a general reference to all parts of the earth, such as verse 6 indicates. "Sea" and "land" occur three times in this passage.

> ▶ *(A)nd he cried out with a loud voice, as when a lion roars; and when he had cried out, seven peals of thunder uttered their voices [Revelation 10:3].*

A lion roars before it attacks. The *seven peals of thunder* are a Scriptural device of warning of impending judgment. These may, then, be related to the seven Bowl Judgments of Chapters 15-16 that will complete God's judgments. John must prophesy of them later in verse 11, but not now. These peals of thunder should be compared to Psalm 29:4-9, which describes the power of the voice of God.

(b) John was forbidden to write about the peals of thunder.

> ▶ *When the seven peals of thunder had spoken, I was about to write; and I heard a voice from heaven saying, "Seal up the things which the seven peals of thunder have spoken and do not write them" [Revelation 10:4].*

I was about to write, in obedience to Revelation 1:19. *A voice from heaven* could be the same voice from Revelation 4:1, the heavenly Father. *Seal up* can carry the idea "seal up at once" and could be like Daniel 8:26 and 12:1. Daniel 8:26 contains the command to seal, and 12:1 describes the future event when the seal is broken.

> The vision of the evenings and mornings which has been told is true; *but keep the vision secret*, for it pertains to many days in the future .... Now at that time Michael, the great young prince who stands guard over the sons of your people, will arise. And there will be a time of distress such as never occurred since there was a nation until that time; and at that time your people, everyone who is found written in the book, will be rescued [Daniel 8:26; 12:1].

> The *secret things* belong to the LORD our God, but the things revealed belong to us and to our sons forever, that we may observe all the words of this law [Deuteronomy 29:29].

► *Then the angel whom I saw standing on the sea and on the land lifted up his right hand to heaven [Revelation 10:5].*

Lifted up his right hand as in taking an oath.

► *(A)nd swore by him who lives forever and ever, who created heaven and the things in it, and the earth and the things in it, and the sea and the things in it, that there will be delay no longer [Revelation 10:6].*

Swore by Him would be the same as Hebrews 6:13.

For when God made the promise to Abraham, since He could *swear* by no one greater, He *swore* by Himself [Hebrews 6:13].

God is swearing by His own name because there is none greater. *Who created heaven .... and the earth .... and the sea* denotes right of ownership by creation. Satan did not create these things; he has no right to possess them.

In the beginning *God created* the heavens and the earth [Genesis 1:1].

All things *came into being through Him,* and apart from Him nothing *came into being* that has come into being [John 1:3].

For by Him all things *were created,* both in the heavens and on earth, visible and invisible, whether thrones or dominions or rulers or authorities – all things *have been created through Him* and for Him. He is before all things, and in Him all things hold together [Colossians 1:16, 17].

God created *all things* through the Person of Jesus Christ. Note that this verse alone totally invalidates the Theory of Evolution.

Delay no longer is translated *time no longer* in the KJV. "Delay no longer" is the better translation. Additionally, the Greek *chronos*, which gives our English word "chronology," used here, is used elsewhere in Scripture to refer to delay. But, it appears in compound with *ouketi*, which means "no longer." Hence, literally "time no longer" or "no more time."

> For yet in a very little while, He who is coming will come, and will not *delay* [Hebrews 10:37].

> For the vision is yet for the appointed time; it hastens toward the goal and will not fail. Though it tarries, wait for it [Habakkuk 2:3].

The *delay* refers to the judgments of God.

> ► *(B)ut in the days of the voice of the seventh angel, when he is about to sound, then the mystery of God is finished, as He preached to His servants the prophets [Revelation 10:7].*

The days of the voice of the seventh angel are further described in Revelation 11:15 and following. These judgments are from God, as He conquers earth in preparation for the reign of Christ on earth. The voice of the seventh angel is when He sounds His trumpet.

... then the mystery of God is finished, that is, the mystery of the Kingdom of God (Revelation 11:16, 17) is finished. God's Kingdom will have been revealed because He is establishing it on earth. The Greek, *musterion,* is that which is previously not revealed.

Preached is *euangelizo*, which gives our word "evangelize," or "preach the Good News" of Jesus dying on the cross for our sins. *Servants* is *doulos*, meaning a willing servant. *Prophets* is *prophatas*, a "spokesman for another."

(c) John was commanded to write the details of God's judgment.

> ► *Then the voice which I heard from heaven, I heard again speaking with me, and saying, "Go, take the*

*book which is open in the hand of the angel who stands
on the sea and on the land" [Revelation 10:8].*

Go, take the book shows that this book was for John, for his benefit, to
prepare him for more prophecy from God.

▶ *So I went to the angel, telling him to give me the
little book. And he said to me, "Take it and eat it; it
will make your stomach bitter, but in your mouth it will
be sweet as honey" [Revelation 10:9].*

Take it and eat it is Biblical symbolism for hearing and appropriating
God's word.

Your words were found and *I ate them,* and Your
words became for me a joy and the delight of my heart;
for I have been called by Your name, O LORD God of
hosts [Jeremiah 15:16].

Now you, son of man, listen to what I am speaking to
you; do not be rebellious like that rebellious house.
Open your mouth and *eat* what I am giving you ...."
Then He said to me, "Son of man, *eat* what you find;
eat this scroll, and go, speak to the house of Israel." So
I opened my mouth, and he fed me this scroll. He said
to me, "Son of man, *feed* your stomach and fill your
body with this scroll which I am giving you." Then I
ate it, and it was sweet as honey in my mouth [Ezekiel
2:8; 3:1-3].

This is the bread that came down from out of heaven,
so that one may *eat* of it and not die. I am the living
bread that came down out of heaven; if anyone *eats* of
this bread, he will live forever; and the bread also
which I will give for the life of the world is My flesh
[John 6:50-51].

God's Word is **bitter** because it tells of divine wrath (in the Tribulation,
first, one-fourth will die, then another one-third will perish). It is also

sweet because it also tells of God's love and grace and mercy and promises and justice, which vindicates who He is.

> How sweet are Your words to my taste! Yes, sweeter than honey to my mouth! From Your precepts I get understanding; therefore I hate every false way [Psalm 119:103, 104].

> ▶ *I took the little book out of the angel's hand and ate it, and in my mouth it was sweet as honey; and when I had eaten it, my stomach was made bitter [Revelation 10:10].*

John had a physical reaction to the Word of God.

> ▶ *And they said to me, "You must prophesy again concerning many peoples and nations and tongues and kings" [Revelation 10:11].*

Many is *pollois*, which emphasizes greatness of size and number.

(2) God sends two special witnesses to Jerusalem (Revelation 11:1-19).

God always provides warning before His judgments. Therefore, in the midst of the Tribulation, immediately after the antichrist sets up his own image in the Holy of Holies in the Temple in Jerusalem, God will send two very powerful prophets to Jerusalem to warn the city and the whole world of God's coming judgment.

> Therefore when you see the Abomination of Desolation which was spoken of through Daniel the prophet, *standing in the holy place* .... Let no one in any way deceive you, for it will not come unless the *apostasy comes first*, and the man of lawlessness is revealed, the son of destruction [Matthew 24:15a, 2 Thessalonians 2:3-4].

Interestingly, when the witness of God's two prophets is rejected and they are killed, their death and resurrection set the stage for the last

Trumpet Judgment, the seventh, the preparation for which is described in verses 14-19.

(a) According to God's measurement, Jerusalem is ripe for judgment.

> ▶ *And there was given me a measuring rod like a staff; and someone said, "Rise and measure the temple of God, and the altar, and those who worship in it" [Revelation 11:1].*

Then is a conjunction that ties this chapter with Chapter 10, which prepared John for more of the Revelation. *A measuring rod* was typically grown in the Jordan River Valley and was 10 feet in length. *A staff* was in some cases a sign of authority as the rod is here. *Get up and measure* was an act of judgment, an act of discernment to see if it is fit for God to dwell there (see Zechariah 2, Ezekiel 40-43 and Revelation 21).

The temple of God in Jerusalem in John's day had been destroyed by Titus of Rome in A.D. 70. Therefore, this temple of God, to be built during the tribulation period, will be the third built by the Jews. It will not "measure up" because the antichrist will have desecrated it with an idol. When this "tribulation temple" is built, it will be dedicated to God, but will be taken over by Satan (see Matthew 24:15-21).

The altar is the "golden altar," the last altar mentioned in Revelation 8:3, which represented the prayers of the saints. However, by this time in the Tribulation the "worshippers" are Christ-rejectors and are praying to the image of the beast. Those who worship in this temple are the Jewish priests during the Tribulation who are apostates and have been deceived by the false prophet (see Revelation 13:11-18). Neither do these priests measure up. This temple cannot be used by Jesus Christ when He returns to earth (Chapter 19), therefore, it becomes subject to the wrath of God.

The beast will then force Muslims, Hindus, Buddhists, Jews and all members of all religions of the world to worship him.

> ▶ *Leave out the court which is outside the temple and do not measure it, for it has been given to the nations;*

and they will tread under foot the holy city for forty-two months [Revelation 11:2].

Technically, *the temple* included only the Holy Place and the Holy of Holies. In his prophecy, Ezekiel saw the court measured as well, because it was the temple and city that Messiah would live in. Here, the temple did *not* measure up, so there is no need to measure the court. Furthermore, the court has been *given to the nations*, *ethnos*, or Gentiles, who will tread it and the city under foot for *forty-two months*, or the last half of the Tribulation. While the verse does not specify which half of the Tribulation, the preceding chapters and the context of this chapter strongly support this as the *last half* of the Tribulation, or what Jesus called "the Great Tribulation."

> For then there will be a *great tribulation*, such as has not occurred since the beginning of the world until now, nor ever will [Matthew 24:21].

Scripture predicts that Jerusalem will fall under the control of the Gentiles.

> So now let Me tell you what I am going to do to My vineyard: I will remove its hedge and it will be consumed; I will break down its wall and it will become trampled ground [Isaiah. 5:5].

> Your holy people possessed Your sanctuary for a little while, our adversaries have trodden it down [Isaiah. 63:18].

This control began with the Babylonian Captivity in 606 B.C. Then, in the New Testament, Jesus and the apostle Paul predicted the cessation of that control.

> (A)nd they will fall by the edge of the sword, and will be led captive into all the nations; and Jerusalem will be *trampled under foot by the Gentiles* until the times of the Gentiles be fulfilled [Luke 21:24].

For I do not want you, brethren, to be uninformed of this mystery – so that you will not be wise in your own estimation – that a partial hardening has happened to Israel until the *fulness of the Gentiles* has come in [Romans 11:25].

(b) God sends two powerful witnesses against Jerusalem.

> ► *And I will grant authority to My two witnesses, and they will prophesy for twelve hundred and sixty days, clothed in sackcloth [Revelation 11:3].*

This passage "flashes back" all the way to the beginning of the Tribulation. The two witnesses prophesy during the first half, and then are killed by the antichrist when he takes over the temple at the mid-point of the Tribulation. Perhaps God uses these two witnesses to convert the 144,000 whom He seals in Revelation 7:4.

I will grant shows God's sovereign control over the situation in Jerusalem. *Authority* is in italics and does not occur in the Greek text. *To My two witnesses* is in the dative case, so God does give something to them. *My* ties all the way back to "the strong angel" of Revelation 10:1, which is most probably Jesus Christ. *Two* is the number of witnessing in the Bible. *Witnesses* is *martus*, which was a judicial witness (one who would swear - to the death - of a truth); hence, our English word *martyr*.

Will prophesy is from *propheteuo*, which means to be the authoritarian spokesman for another. *Twelve hundred and sixty days* is the exact length of their ministry, so if the unbelievers knew of short-term prophecy, they could easily tell that these men were from God. *Sackcloth* is the Biblical sign of mourning and humility and repentance. Both Daniel and John the Baptist wore sackcloth as they identified with the sins of the people.

> ► *These are the two olive trees and two lampstands that stand before the Lord of the earth [Revelation 11:4].*

The *two olive trees and the two lampstands* according to Zechariah 4:3-14 are two witnesses from God.

Olive trees gave the olives that gave the oil for the lamps; the lampstand gave the light, which is the Word of God.

> Your word is a *lamp* to my feet and a *light* to my path [Psalm 119:105].

The Lord of the earth declares God's right to rule over the earth, not Satan's. Satan has no right to rule.

> ► *And if anyone wants to harm them, fire flows out of their mouth and devours their enemies; so if anyone wants to harm them, he must be killed in this way [Revelation 11:5].*

Fire flows out of their mouth may be taken literally, or perhaps it may happen as with Elijah in 2 Kings 1 where he spoke the words and fire fell from heaven. *In this way* is a very specific form of punishment that removes all doubt that these men are from God and that they have great power.

Verses 5 and 6 are very similar to the ministries of Elijah and Moses of the Old Testament, the only two prophets whose ministries were unfinished. Some hold that these two witnesses are Moses and Elijah.

> ► *These have the power to shut up the sky, so that rain will not fall during the days of their prophesying; and they have power over the waters to turn them into blood, and to strike the earth with every plague, as often as they desire [Revelation 11:6].*

For *shut up the sky* see 2 Kings 17 where Elijah prayed and it did not rain in Israel for three and one-half years, the same length of the last half of the Tribulation. In 2 Kings we are not told of the length of the drought until Jesus reveals it in Luke's gospel.

> But I say to you in truth there were many widows in Israel in the days of Elijah, when the sky was shut up

for *three years and six months*, when a great famine came over all the land [Luke 4:25].

For *into blood,*

Thus says the LORD, "By this you shall know that I am the LORD: behold, I will strike the water that is in the Nile with the staff that is in my hand, and it will be *turned to blood"* [Exodus 7:17].

Strike the earth shows that their ministry reaches outside Jerusalem.

(c) The beast kills God's two witnesses.

▶ *When they have finished their testimony, the beast that comes up out of the abyss will make war with them, and overcome them and kill them [Revelation 11:7].*

When they have finished is up to God, not Satan.

For I am already being poured out as a drink offering, and the time of my departure has come. I have fought the good fight, I have *finished the course*, I have kept the faith; in the future there is laid up for me the crown of righteousness, which the Lord, the righteous Judge, will award to me on that day; and not only to me, but also to all who have loved His appearing [Paul, (2 Timothy 4:6-8)].

Satan can kill God's messengers, but he cannot kill the message. This is the first time *the beast* occurs in the book; he will appear some 36 times. The Greek is *tharion*, which means a beast, a wild animal, a brutish man. *That comes up out of the abyss* shows this to be a demon-possessed man, possessed by the Devil himself. *Overcome and kill them* makes this look as if Satan is more powerful than God, but God is simply allowing this to happen because the work of His witnesses is now finished.

▶ *And their dead bodies will lie in the street of the great city which mystically is called Sodom and Egypt, where also their Lord was crucified [Revelation 11:8].*

Bodies will lie in the street shows the brutal, inhuman attitude of the beast and his followers. *The great city* is none other than Jerusalem herself. *Sodom and Egypt* were deserving of God's judgments when they finally came. Jerusalem is here compared to Sodom for its immorality and to Egypt for its idolatry. Worshipping the beast will be spiritual immorality and idolatry.

Their Lord was crucified is obviously the Lord Jesus Christ. God never asks us to do anything He won't do Himself. As Jesus died for all of us on the cross, the two witnesses die for their testimony to Christ.

And Jesus came up and spoke to them, saying, *"All authority has been given to Me* in heaven and on earth" [Matthew 28:18].

(S)o at the name of Jesus every knee will bow, of those who are in heaven and on earth and under the earth, and that every tongue will confess that *Jesus Christ is Lord,* to the glory of God the Father [Philippians 2:10,11].

▶ *Those from the peoples and tribes and tongues and nations will look at their dead bodies for three and a half days, and will not permit their dead bodies to be laid in a tomb [Revelation 11:9].*

Peoples and tribes and tongues and nations reveal the worldwide rebellion against God as in the days of Noah.

But of that day and hour no one knows, not even the angels of heaven, nor the Son, but the Father alone. For the coming of the Son of Man will be *just like the days of Noah.* For as in those days before the flood they were eating and drinking, marrying and giving in marriage, until the day that Noah entered the ark [Matthew 24:36-38].

The people will no longer fear God, and will have become part of Satan's rebellion. Sadly, they will not realize that Satan cannot give them eternal life and that he has only used them to gain his own selfish objectives.

Ironically, *three and a half days* are symbolic of the first half (the first three and a half years) of the Tribulation, all of which verifies God's perfect and absolute control over the entire situation. Every *people, tribe, tongue, and nation will look on their bodies* could not be fulfilled without the prior invention and development of modern imaging technology. *Will not permit their dead bodies to be laid in a tomb* parallels the custom of crucifixion in the days of Jesus, where the bodies were left to hang on the crosses.

> ▶ *And those who dwell on the earth will rejoice over them and celebrate; and they will send gifts to one another, because these two prophets tormented those who dwell on the earth [Revelation 11:10].*

Those who dwell on the earth occurs several times in the Book of the Revelation and emphasizes the limitation of their lives only to this present life.

Rejoice ... celebrate ... send gifts are all indicative of the "pleasures of sin for a season," but they will soon pay for this sin.

> (C)hoosing rather to endure ill-treatment with the people of God than to enjoy the passing *pleasures of sin* [Hebrews 11:25].

Tormented is the verb *basanizo*, from *basanos*, the lapis stone from Lydia used in trying metals; hence, to try someone or examine them or torment them. In our context the tormenting was with a message (see Revelation 20:10 where the same verb is used).

(d) God resurrects and raptures His two witnesses.

> ▶ *But after the three and a half days, the breath of life from God came into them, and they stood on their feet;*

and great fear fell upon those who were watching them [Revelation 11:11].

The breath of life are the same Greek words as in the Septuagint, the Greek translation of the Old Testament.

Then the LORD God formed man of the dust of the ground, and breathed into his nostrils *the breath of life*; and man became a living being [Genesis 2:7].

From God is literally "out of God," a genitive of source. ***Those who were watching them*** were the unbelievers because the believers had all run for their lives.

Therefore when you see the Abomination of Desolation which was spoken of through Daniel the prophet, standing in the Holy Place (let the reader understand), then those who are in Judea *must flee* to the mountains [Matthew 24:15, 16].

▶ *And they heard a loud voice from heaven saying to them, "Come up here." Then they went up into heaven in the cloud, and their enemies watched them [Revelation 11:12].*

Come up here was the same command God gave John back in verse one of Chapter 4. ***In the cloud*** was like Christ's ascension in Acts 1:9. ***Their enemies watched them*** will not be like the Rapture, which will take place in an instant of time.

(I)n a moment, in the twinkling of an eye, at the last trumpet; for the trumpet will sound, and the dead will be *raised imperishable*, and we will be changed [1 Corinthians 15:52].

Then we who are alive and remain will be *caught up together* with them in the clouds to meet the Lord in the air, and so we shall always be with the Lord [1 Thessalonians 4:17].

► *And in that hour there was a great earthquake, and a tenth of the city fell; seven thousand people were killed in the earthquake, and the rest were terrified and gave glory to the God of heaven [Revelation 11:13].*

The rest are the survivors of the earthquake. **Gave glory to the God of heaven** does not mean that they have been converted. They are simply terrified!

(e) Rejection of God's two witnesses brings on the seventh Trumpet Judgment.

[1] The eagle warns of the third woe, which is the seventh trumpet.

► *The second woe is past; behold, the third woe is coming quickly [Revelation 11:14].*

The second woe, according to Revelation 8:13, 9:1, and 9:13, is the sixth trumpet judgment. Therefore, the "third woe" must be the seventh Trumpet Judgment, which actually contains the Seven Bowl Judgments of Chapters 15 and 16. Time for planet earth has now grown critically short.

[2] The seventh Trumpet sounding brings voices from heaven, announcing God's Kingdom on earth.

► *Then the seventh angel sounded; and there were loud voices in heaven, saying, "The kingdom of the world has become the kingdom of our Lord and of His Christ; and He will reign forever and ever" [Revelation 11:15].*

Voices is plural, which before in the Book of the Revelation has usually been singular. **Kingdom** in the KJV is plural based on a different Greek manuscript. The singular suggests that the antichrist has been successful in forming a one-world government.

Has become is what we call a futuristic perfect tense; perfect tense is past action with present ongoing results; it is futuristic because it is so certain that God refers to it with a past-tense verb.

He will reign forever and ever does not contradict the Millennium taught in Revelation 20:1-10. The Millennium is simply the beginning of Christ's eternal reign. The Millennium, literally one thousand years (Revelation 20:1-3), is God's final dispensation before the final judgment (Revelation 20:11-15). However, God promised King David in 2 Samuel 7:16 that his kingdom will be forever.

> Your house and your kingdom shall endure before Me *forever*; your throne shall be established *forever* [2 Samuel 7:16].

Therefore, the Millennium, with Jesus ruling on David's throne in Jerusalem, is simply the beginning of an eternal, earthly kingdom.

> ▶ *And the twenty-four elders, who sit on their thrones before God, fell on their faces and worshiped God, saying, "We give You thanks, O Lord God, the Almighty, who are and who were, because You have taken Your great power and have begun to reign"* [Revelation 11:16, 17].

Almighty is *pantokrator*, which is all authority, using the prefix *pan*, meaning "all;" and *power* is *dunamis*, (which gives our word *dynamite*), the ability to exercise that authority (see also Psalm 2).

> ▶ *And the nations were enraged, and Your wrath came, and the time came for the dead to be judged, and the time to reward Your bond-servants the prophets and saints and those who fear Your name, the small and the great, and to destroy those who destroy the earth* [Revelation 11:18].

Were enraged is an aorist indicative passive from *orgizo*, the same root for "wrath." Man's wrath is potent, but God's wrath is omnipotent.

The *dead* probably refers to the spiritually dead, and *judged* is *krino*, meaning to separate.

> And you were dead in your trespasses and sins [Ephesians 2:1].

And then I will declare to them, "I never knew you; depart from Me, you who practice lawlessness" [Matthew 7:23].

Those who destroy the earth are the unbelieving survivors of the Tribulation.

[3] God prepares to unleash His wrath upon the earth.

> ▶ *And the temple of God which is in heaven was opened; and the ark of His covenant appeared in His temple, and there were flashes of lightning and sounds and peals of thunder and an earthquake and a great hailstorm [Revelation 11:19].*

This phrase, *the ark of His covenant* appears only here in all of Holy Scripture.

Now come signs of divine indignation.

(3) The dragon (Satan), tries to destroy Christ and the woman (the nation Israel), Revelation 12:1-17.

Chapters 12 and 13 are very important. They include nine personages or groups to describe the intense struggle over who will rule the universe. These nine personages are:

(a) The *woman*, symbolic of the nation Israel, Revelation 12:1-2.
(b) The *dragon*, symbolic of Satan, Revelation 12:3.
(c) The *child* symbolic of Jesus Christ, Revelation 12:4-5.
(d) *God* the Father, Revelation 12:5-6.
(e) *Michael* the archangel, Revelation 12:7.
(f) The holy *angels*, Revelation 2:7.
(g) The unholy or *fallen angels*, Revelation 12:7-9.
(h) The first beast or *antichrist*, Revelation 13:1.
(i) The second beast or the *false prophet*, Revelation 13:11.

Chapters 12 and 13, especially Chapter 12, describe valuable details of what theologians call the "Angelic Conflict," the war that has been raging between God and Satan ever since Satan rebelled and lost his estate, his standing, and his ministry before God. By comparing Genesis 1:1-2 and Job 38:1-7, it can be concluded that the fall of Satan was probably while God was creating the earth and the universe. At the laying of the foundation of the earth (see Job 38:4 and 7) all the sons of God sang (sons of God being a reference to the holy angels, including Lucifer before he rebelled). But in Genesis 1:2, the earth was *tohu waw bohu*, Hebrew for "formless and void." This phrase in the Hebrew is always used to denote some catastrophic event. It is safe to conclude that Lucifer rebelled when he saw "the heavens and the earth" that God created, and wanted to rule over them.

(a) In the "Angelic Conflict," Satan tried to destroy Christ at His birth. (Matthew's Gospel records King Herod's attempt to kill Jesus by slaughtering all the male children in Bethlehem.)

> Then when Herod saw that he had been tricked by the maji, he became very enraged, and sent and *slew all the male children* who were in Bethlehem and its vicinity, from two years old and under, according to the time which he had determined from the maji [Matthew 2:16].

> ► *A great sign appeared in heaven: a woman clothed with the sun, and the moon under her feet, and on her head a crown of twelve stars; and she was with child; and she cried out, being in labor and in pain to give birth [Revelation 12:1,2].*

Sign is *semeion*, which is an attesting miracle, something given to show an important truth. The same word occurs in verse 3.

In heaven is where the "sign" appeared to show the origin of God's revelation and plan, but the outworking of God's will is on the earth, because that is where the Christ was born. *Woman ... twelve stars* according to Genesis 37:9-11 is a description of the nation Israel. *The sun* was Jacob, the *moon* was Rachel, and the *twelve stars* are the twelve brothers who were the heads of the twelve tribes of Israel.

> Now he had still another dream, and related it to his brothers, and said, "Lo, I have had still another dream;

and behold, the sun and the moon and eleven stars were bowing down to me." He related it to his father and to his brothers; and his father rebuked him and said to him, "What is this dream that you have had? Shall I and your mother and your brothers actually come to bow ourselves down before you to the ground?" [Genesis 37:9-10].

Crown is *stephanos*, an earned crown, not to be confused with the *diadamata,* which belongs to the heir, Jesus Christ, Revelation 19:12, and which Satan counterfeits in Revelation 12:3 with the antichrist.

Woman, she, and *she* are used for the nation because she will bring forth a man-child, a Messiah. *Cried out* describes the pain and anguish which Israel has suffered over the centuries because she brought forth the Messiah.

▶ *Then another sign appeared in heaven: and behold, a great red dragon having seven heads and ten horns, and on his head were seven diadems [Revelation 12:3].*

Another is *allos*, another of the same kind or magnitude; one of equal significance. *Red* is the same color as the horse in Revelation 6:4 that signified war. The great dragon is a dragon of *war! Seven* is the number of completion or perfection and so here Satan again counterfeits God.

The *seven heads and ten horns* are an exact description of the revived Roman Empire that the antichrist will use to rise to world power. These nations, which the antichrist will rule, can come from Europe or from the Middle East; all of which at one time were under Roman rule.

After this I kept looking in the night visions, and behold, a fourth beast, dreadful and terrifying and extremely strong; and it had large iron teeth. It devoured and crushed and trampled down the remainder with its feet; and it was different from all the beasts that were before it, and it had *ten horns*. While I was contemplating the horns, behold, another horn, a little one, came up among them, and three of the first horns were pulled out by the roots before it; and behold, this horn possessed eyes like the eyes of a man and a mouth uttering great boasts [Daniel 7:7,8].

See also Revelation 13:1, which introduces the first beast.

> ► *And his tail swept away a third of the stars of heaven and threw them to the earth. And the dragon stood before the woman who was about to give birth, so that when she gave birth he might devour her child [Revelation 12:4].*

A third of the stars of heaven refers to angels that Satan deceived and dragged with him in his rebellion against God. They chose to rebel, and now they must pay the consequences - Satan *threw them to the earth.* Satan is using them to help him try to defeat Christ. While Chapters 10-14 give further details of the Tribulation, this chapter gives details all the way back to the creation of the world. *Stood* is a perfect tense, past action with present, on-going results; Satan had been standing a long time to try to destroy Christ when He was born in Bethlehem.

> Then when Herod saw that he had been tricked by the maji, he became very enraged, and sent and *slew all the male children* who were in Bethlehem and all its vicinity, from two years old and under, according to the time which he had determined from the maji ... But when Herod died, behold, an angel of the Lord appeared in a dream to Joseph in Egypt, and said, "Get up, take the Child and His mother, and go into the land of Israel; for those who sought the Child's life are dead [Matthew 2:16, 19, 20].

Regarding *he might devour her child;*

> And I will put enmity between you and the woman, and between your seed and her seed; He shall bruise you on the head, and you shall bruise him on the heel .... Therefore, since the children share in flesh and blood, He Himself likewise also partook of the same, that through death He might render powerless him who

had the power of death, that is, the devil .... and concerning judgment, because the ruler of this world has been judged [Genesis 3:15; Hebrews 2:14; John 16:11].

Christ knew that the way to life (with God) is through death (on the cross).

> ► *And she gave birth to a son, a male child, who is to rule all the nations with a rod of iron; and her child was caught up to God and to His throne [Revelation 12:5].*

Son (Greek *huios*) and **male** (Greek *arsen*), equal a male child. **Rule all the nations with a rod of iron** will occur in the Millennium (see Psalm 2 and Revelation 19:15). **Was caught up to God** describes the resurrection and ascension of Christ, the evidence of His victory. **Caught up** is *harpazo*, the same word used in 1 Thessalonians 4:17 and 2 Corinthians 12:2.

> Then we who are alive and remain will be *caught up* together with them in the clouds to meet the Lord in the air, and so we shall always be with the Lord [1 Thessalonians 4:17].

> I know a man in Christ who fourteen years ago – whether in the body I do not know, or out of the body I do not know, God knows – such a man was *caught up* to the third heaven [2 Corinthians 12:2].

(b) In the Angelic Conflict, Satan will lose his access to the third heaven.

> ► *Then the woman fled into the wilderness where she had a place prepared by God, so that there she would be nourished for one thousand two hundred and sixty days [Revelation 12:6].*

For **wilderness;**

> Therefore, behold, I will allure her, bring her into the *wilderness* and speak kindly to her. Then I will give her vineyards from there, and the valley of Achor as a door of hope. And she will sing there as in the days of her youth, as in the day when she came up from the land of Egypt [Hosea 2:14-15].

Nourish is *trepho*, which means to feed, to cherish, to pamper (as with manna in the wilderness, or when God took care of Elijah in the wilderness).

> ► *And there was war in heaven, Michael and his angels waging war with the dragon. The dragon and his angels waged war [Revelation 12:7].*

War in heaven, which Jesus warned about, will be at the mid-point of the Tribulation.

> Therefore when you see the ABOMINATION OF DESOLATION which was spoken of through Daniel the prophet, standing in the holy place ... [Matthew 24:15a]

In the first half of the Tribulation, the antichrist will have put up with the Jews, but now he will turn on them violently. *Michael* is the only named "archangel," found in Jude 9. *His angels* are holy, unfallen angels (perhaps Lucifer was the archangel before he fell into sin).

The second *his angels* (the dragon's) are obviously unholy, fallen angels.

> ► *(A)nd they were not strong enough, and there was no longer a place found for them in heaven [Revelation 12:8].*

In heaven is the Third Heaven, see Job chapters 1-2, where the conversation took place between God and Satan regarding Job. Up until Chapter 12, Satan had access to the third heaven.

▶ *And the great dragon was thrown down, the serpent of old who is called the devil and Satan, who deceives the whole world; he was thrown down to the earth, and his angels were thrown down with him [Revelation 12:9].*

Serpent of old dates all the way back to the Garden of Eden. **Devil** is *diabolos*, which means slanderer (see verse 10). **Satan** is the same in Hebrew and Greek, *satan*, or "adversary."

Whole world is *oikoumena*, meaning the whole inhabited earth.

▶ *Then I heard a loud voice in heaven saying, "Now the salvation, and the power, and the kingdom of our God and the authority of His Christ have come, for the accuser of our brethren has been thrown down, he who accuses them before our God day and night [Revelation 12:10].*

A loud voice is probably from the saints in heaven. **The salvation** is *soter*, which means deliverance. **Power** is *dunamis* (see page 132).

Authority is *eksousia*.

And Jesus came up and spoke to them, saying, "All *authority* has been given to Me in heaven and on earth [Matthew 28:18].

For **His Christ** see Revelation 11:15, page 131. Only Christ holds all three Old Testament offices of Prophet, Priest, and King. We can contrast the *false prophet* to Christ as a Prophet; *accuser* to the Priesthood of Christ; and the *antichrist* to the Kingship of Christ.

▶ *And they overcame him because of the blood of the Lamb and because of the word of their testimony, and they did not love their life even when faced with death [Revelation 12:11].*

The **blood** of Christ on the cross is what gives Christ the victory. **Love** is *agapao*, unselfish love, unconditional love.

▶ *For this reason, rejoice, O heavens and you who dwell in them. Woe to the earth and the sea, because the devil has come down to you, having great wrath, knowing that he has only a short time [Revelation 12:12].*

Wrath is not the same word *orga*, which we found in Revelation 11:18 for the wrath of God; here it is *thumos*, which simply describes emotional wrath. **Knowing** is from *oida,* meaning to know intellectually; to know intuitively.

(c) In the continuing Angelic Conflict, Satan will try to annihilate the nation Israel. If Satan could destroy Israel, then God could not fulfill His original promises to Abraham, Isaiah, Jacob, and David. With Israel destroyed, Satan could get to rule the world forever.

▶ *And when the dragon saw that he was thrown down to the earth, he persecuted the woman who gave birth to the male child [Revelation 12:13].*

Zechariah 13:8 predicts that two-thirds of the Jews in the land of Israel who are alive will be killed.

"It will come about in all the land," declares the Lord, "that two parts in it will be cut off and perish; but the third will be left in it" [Zechariah 13:8].

▶ *But the two wings of the great eagle were given to the woman, so that she could fly into the wilderness to her place, where she was nourished for a time and times and half a time, from the presence of the serpent [Revelation 12:14].*

The great eagle may be that of Revelation 8:13 or figurative of God's power to deliver.

You yourselves have seen what I did to the Egyptians, and how I *bore you on eagle's wings*, and brought you to Myself [Exodus 19:4].

Like an eagle that stirs up its nest, that hovers over its young, He *spread His wings and caught* them, He carried them on His pinions. The Lord alone *guided* him, and there was no foreign god with him [Deut. 32:11,12].

A time and times and half a time is the last 3 and 1/2 years of the Tribulation.

He will speak out against the Most High and wear down the saints of the Highest One, and he will intend to make alterations in times and in law; and they will be given into his hand for a *time, times, and half a time* .... I heard the man dressed in linen, who was above the waters of the river, as he raised his right hand and his left toward heaven, and swore by Him who lives forever that it would be for a *time, times, and half a time*; and as soon as they finish shattering the power of the holy people, all these events will be completed [Daniel 7:25; 12:7].

▶ *And the serpent poured water like a river out of his mouth after the woman, so that he might cause her to be swept away with the flood. But the earth helped the woman, and the earth opened its mouth and drank up the river which the dragon poured out of his mouth [Revelation 12:15, 16].*

These verses might be referring to literal events, describing how the power of Satan tries to flood the valleys of the escaping Jews, or it may be figurative to describe the campaign to annihilate them.

▶ *So the dragon was enraged with the woman, and went off to make war with the rest of her children, who keep the commandments of God and hold to the testimony of Jesus [Revelation 12:17].*

The rest is probably the believing remnant of the Jews.

(4) Satan, the beast, and the false prophet (the *unholy* trinity), will take over the whole world, Revelation 13:1-18.

The devil always imitates God, who exists in the form of three Divine Persons, or the *Holy* Trinity. Satan acts as God the Father; antichrist acts as God the Son; and the false prophet acts as God the Holy Spirit. Satan masterminds the plot to take over the world.

The antichrist will attempt to carry out that plan; the false prophet will try to point all people of the world to worship him (antichrist, the first beast). While Satan has always been on earth, the antichrist and false prophet will become known at the onset of the Tribulation (Revelation 6:2), but their roles will dramatically increase to world domination in the last half of the Tribulation, which is the primary thrust of chapter 13.

(a) The first beast (the antichrist) will politically rule the world.

[1] The beast will be very powerful, receiving his power from Satan.

> ▶ *And the dragon stood on the sand of the seashore. Then I saw a beast coming up out of the sea, having ten horns and seven heads, and on his horns were ten diadems, and on his heads were blasphemous names [Revelation 13:1].*

The dragon in the New American Standard reads "I" in the King James and "the dragon" in the NIV. The textual variance leans toward the NASV/NIV readings, which would refer then to the beast, not to John. *Beast* is the same *tharion* in Revelation 11:7, which means wild animal, monster, brutish man, a bully.

The sea, as in Revelation 10:2, probably refers to the nations of Gentiles. This first beast (as in verse 12) has been around since Revelation 6:1-2, the early part of the Tribulation. *Seven heads* refer to the kings or heads of the seven nations left of the original ten after antichrist takes over.

> After this I kept looking in the night visions, and behold, a fourth beast, dreadful and terrifying and

extremely strong; and it had large iron teeth. It devoured and crushed and trampled down the remainder with its feet; and it was different from all the beasts that were before it, and it had ten horns. While I was contemplating the horns, behold, another horn, a little one, came up among them, and three of the first horns were pulled out by the roots before it; and behold, this horn possessed eyes like the eyes of a man and a mouth uttering great boasts [Daniel 7:7,8].

Ten diadems, then, refers to the ten kingdoms of the Ten Nation Confederation, also referred to as the Revived Roman Empire. *Blasphemous* is from the Greek *blasphemia,* which is calumny (false accusation of a crime or offense), railing, verbal reproach. In Scripture, blasphemy is aimed at God and His name. It occurs again in verses 5 and 6.

> ► *And the beast which I saw was like a leopard, and his feet were like those of a bear, and his mouth like the mouth of a lion. And the dragon gave him his power and his throne and great authority [Revelation 13:2].*

Like sets up an analogy or simile. *Leopard* is swift, like the ancient Greek empire under Alexander. *Bear* is powerful like the ancient Medo-Persian Empire under Cyrus and Darius. *Lion* is regal and ferocious like the ancient Babylonian Empire under Nebuchadnezzar. This first beast will have the combined wisdom and strength of those ancient kings. *The dragon* is Satan himself, Revelation 12:9.

Power is *dunamis,* and *authority* is *eksousia,* the same words in Revelation 12:10 used to describe God.

[2] The world will worship Satan and the beast.

> ► *I saw one of his heads as if it had been slain, and his fatal wound was healed. And the whole earth was amazed and followed after the beast [Revelation 13:3].*

Seven heads and ten diadems (see verse 1) refer to the Revived Roman Empire, so *one of his heads* must refer to the antichrist himself, who receives a mortal wound. This imagery could also be referring to the seeming death of the Roman Empire, only to be revived in the last days. The antichrist receives this fatal wound (of a sword, verses 12 and 14), and Satan heals him. *Fatal wound* is the Greek *thanatos*, which is literally "death." *The whole earth* is the first reference to the entire world going after the beast, but they now do so because they begin to see him as a god.

> ► *(T)hey worshipped the dragon because he gave his authority to the beast; and they worshipped the beast saying, "Who is like the beast, and who is able to wage war with him?" [Revelation 13:4].*

Hence, they *worshiped the dragon*; they *proskeuneo* (Revelation 11:16), or "kissed the hand towards." It is the Greek picture of kneeling down before someone to kiss their hand.

> Now therefore, O kings, show discernment; take warning, O judges of the earth. Worship the LORD with reverence and rejoice with trembling. Do homage to the Son, that He not become angry, and you perish in the way, for His wrath may soon be kindled. How blessed are all who take refuge in Him! [Psalm 2:10-12].

This is what Satan has always wanted - all of mankind to fall down and worship him. This is what he has been working towards for centuries! Their question means, "not even God can *wage war* with the beast and the dragon!"

[3] The beast and his kingdom will oppose God and His Kingdom.

> ► *There was given to him a mouth speaking arrogant words and blasphemies, and authority to act for forty-two months was given to him [Revelation 13:5].*

Arrogant words are further representative of the pride of this beast, similarly described in Daniel's prophecy.

While I was contemplating the horns, behold, another horn, a little one, came up among them, and three of the first horns were pulled out by the roots before it; and behold, this horn possessed eyes like the eyes of a man and a mouth uttering *great boasts* .... Then I kept looking because of the sound of the *boastful words* which the horn was speaking; I kept looking until the beast was slain, and its body was destroyed and given to the burning fire .... He will *speak out against* the Most High and wear down the saints of the Highest One, and he will intend to make alterations in times and in law; and they will be given into his hand for a time, times, and half a time [Daniel 7:8, 11, 25].

The *forty-two months* are the last half of the Tribulation.

> ▶ *And he opened his mouth in blasphemies against God, to blaspheme His name and His tabernacle, that is, those who dwell in heaven [Revelation 13:6].*

His **blasphemies** are aimed at God, God's **tabernacle** (*skana, dwelling place*), and God's people (compare God's authority over heaven and earth, Genesis 1:1 and Revelation 1:5, 11:15, and 12:10).

> ▶ *It was also given to him to make war with the saints and to overcome them, and authority over every tribe and people and tongue and nation was given to him [Revelation 13:7].*

It was given to him, that is by Satan. *The saints* are the *hagioi*, or "holy ones," "set apart ones" (set apart by trusting in Christ; not set apart by their own worthiness). *Overcome* is *nikao*, which is the same word "overcame" in Revelation 12:11. This gives our English word *nike*, meaning "victory."

Tribe and people and tongue and nation describes the whole world, a common goal or dream of many dictators.

> ... the fourth beast will be a fourth kingdom on the earth, which will be different from all the other

kingdoms and will *devour the whole earth* and tread it down and crush it [Daniel 7:23].

> ► *All who dwell on the earth will worship him, everyone whose name has not been written from the foundation of the world in the book of life of the Lamb who has been slain [Revelation 13:8].*

All is qualified with *whose name has not been written ... in the book of life of the Lamb,* which means all unbelievers in the Tribulation, both unsaved Jews and unsaved Gentiles. Here is a one-world religion! *From the foundation of the world* actually occurs in the Greek text after the word "slain" as in the KJV.

> ► *If anyone has an ear, let him hear [Revelation 13:9].*

This verse omits "to the churches" found several times in Chapters 2 and 3, because the Church was *raptured* between Chapters 3 and 4.

> ► *If anyone is destined for captivity, to captivity he goes; if anyone kills with the sword, with the sword he must be killed. Here is the perseverance and the faith of the saints [Revelation 13:10].*

Is destined for can be read "leads into." *Captivity* and *kills* are descriptions of persecutions of believers during the Tribulation (see Matthew 25:31-46). *The perseverance and the faith* means to wait upon the "vengeance of God."

> Never take your own revenge, beloved, but leave room for the wrath of God, for it is written, *"Vengeance is Mine,* I will repay," says the Lord [Romans 12:19].

(b) The second beast (the false prophet) will religiously rule the world.

[1] Receiving his power from Satan, the second beast (the religious guru of the world), will require the people to worship the first beast, who, by this time, is indwelt by Satan himself.

> ► *Then I saw another beast coming up out of the earth; and he had two horns like a lamb and he spoke as a dragon [Revelation 13:11].*

Another is *allos*, which means another of the same kind. **Beast** is the same word as in verse 1. **The earth** probably refers to the nation Israel, as in Revelation 10:2. Therefore, the false prophet could be a Jew.

Two horns like a lamb describe this second beast as religious. But, the **dragon**, Satan, gives him his words.

> ► *He exercises all the authority of the first beast in his presence. And he makes the earth and those who dwell in it to worship the first beast, whose fatal wound was healed [Revelation 13:12].*

Exercises, makes, performs (see verse 13), and **cause** (see verse 15), are all the same Greek word *poieo*, which means to do, make or cause. If the first beast is not God (and of course he isn't), then this second beast is a false prophet (see Revelation 19:20).

> ► *He performs great signs, so that he even makes fire come down out of heaven to the earth in the presence of men [Revelation 13:13].*

Signs is *semeion*, which means an attesting miracle. **Fire ... out of heaven** is like the two witnesses of God in Revelation 11:5.

[2] The second beast deceives the people into worshipping the first beast.

> ► *And he deceives those who dwell on the earth because of the signs which it was given him to perform in the presence of the beast, telling those who dwell on the earth to make an image to the beast who had the wound of the sword and has come to life [Revelation 13:14].*

Deceives is *planao*, meaning to lead astray (Revelation 12:9). *Image* is *eikon*, which gives our English word icon. This also supports the fact that this man is a false prophet.

> You shall not make for yourself an *idol*, or any likeness of what is in heaven above or on the earth beneath or in the water under the earth. You shall not worship them or serve them; for I, the LORD your God, am a jealous God, visiting the iniquity of the fathers on the children, on the third and the fourth generations of those who hate Me [Exodus 20:4,5].

This image, *eikon*, will be mentioned seven more times.

Has come to life does not mean that Satan has the power to resurrect a man. The aorist tense describes a completed action, "has lived," and is not *anistami*, which is a separate word for resurrection. It simply means *he survived*.

> ► *And it was given to him to give breath to the image of the beast, so that the image of the beast would even speak and cause as many as do not worship the image of the beast to be killed [Revelation 13:15].*

Give breath is *pneuma* translated "life" in the KJV.

[3] The second beast forces people to worship the first beast.

> ► *And he causes all, the small and the great, and the rich and the poor, and the free men and the slaves, to be given a mark on their right hand or on their forehead [Revelation 13:16].*

All social levels are described. *Mark* is *charagma*, from *charasso*, to notch, engrave, impress, make an exact impression.

> ► *(A)nd he provides that no one will be able to buy or sell, except the one who has the mark, either the name of the beast or the number of his name [Revelation 13:17].*

Name or *number* shows it is an identifying mark.

> ► *Here is wisdom. Let him who has understanding calculate the number of the beast, for the number is that of a man; and his number is six hundred and sixty-six [Revelation 13:18].*

Greek letters have numerical value; the letters of the name "Jesus," for example, total **888.** The name of the beast will total **666;** the number 6 is the number in Scripture for man, short of Deity. It is also the number for man in rebellion against God.

(5) Christ seals the 144,000 and spiritually triumphs over the unholy trinity, Revelation 14:1-20.

Remember that Chapters 10-14 are a parenthesis which give added detail to both halves of the Tribulation during which the Seal and Trumpet Judgments are taking place, which were introduced in Chapters 6, 8, and 9. In Chapters 11-13, the two witnesses of God are killed by the antichrist, all part of the Angelic Conflict, which has Satan trying to annihilate the nation Israel (Chapter 12), and the antichrist and the false prophet taking over the whole world (Chapter 13). It might seem that Satan will win the battle, but Chapter 14 prophesys that Christ will be triumphant over the devil and his followers. Christ will defeat the unholy trinity.

(a) At the end of the Tribulation, the 144,000 are still alive.

> ► *Then I looked, and behold, the Lamb was standing on Mount Zion, and with Him one hundred and forty-four thousand, having His name and the name of His Father written on their foreheads [Revelation 14:1].*

The Lamb has the definite article, and refers to the Lord Jesus Christ ... in contrast to the false prophet back in Revelation 13:11, who appeared "*like* a lamb."

Mount Zion is Jerusalem and Jesus is *standing on it!* This shows that Christ has triumphantly been working on earth and is about to establish His government in Jerusalem. And who is with Him in this triumphal scene but the same *one hundred and forty-four thousand* whom He sealed back in Revelation 7:3-8. They were sealed to be spared by the attacks of antichrist, and here they are at the end of the Tribulation, still alive.

Having ... written is a perfect passive participle, past action with present, on-going results. The past action of being sealed has preserved their lives and ministries throughout the Tribulation. Here, we learn what the seal was - *the name of His Father* - which the false prophet counterfeited back in Revelation 13:17 where Christ-rejectors could receive either the name of the beast or the number of his name. Notice that the "name of His Father" is not given.

> ▶ *And I heard a voice from heaven like the sound of many waters and like the sound of loud thunder, and the voice which I heard was like the sound of harpists playing on their harps [Revelation 14:2].*

A voice is one of seven times this voice is heard from heaven in the Book of the Revelation. In Revelation 14:13 the voice is identified as the voice of the Holy Spirit, therefore, in Revelation 10:4 and 8; 11:12; 14:2 and 13; 18:4 and 21:3, it may be the voice of the Holy Spirit. Or, as in Revelation 1:10 and 15, it may be the voice of Jesus Himself.

Like occurs three times as John tries to describe the voice, which is very similar to Jesus in Chapter 1. It was loud like many waters, deep like loud thunder and melodious like harps playing. *Harps* is *kathara*, which was a lyre, a harp-like instrument with two curved arms, a yoke, and 4 to 10 strings that were stroked with a plectrum or pick.

> ▶ *And they sang a new song before the throne and before the four living creatures and the elders; and no one could learn the song except the one hundred and forty-four thousand who had been purchased from the earth [Revelation 14:3].*

They has the 144,000 as its nearest antecedent. The difficulty is that "they" sang *before the throne and before the four living creatures and the elders*, who are all in the Third Heaven back in Revelation 7:9-17. Verse 1 said that the 144,000 were standing on Mt. Zion, which is on earth. The difficulty is eliminated when we exegete the word *before*, *enopion*, "in the eyes of" or "in the sight of," or "to." *Who had been purchased from the earth* is by the precious blood of Jesus Christ; there is no self-justification in God's salvation.

> And He said to them, "You are those who justify yourselves in the sight of men, but God knows your hearts; for that which is highly esteemed among men is detestable in the sight of God" [Luke 16:15].

No one could learn the song except the 144,000 because in Revelation 5:9-10 the elders had their own song, and in Revelation 7:10 the martyrs had their own song. *Had been purchased* is a perfect passive participle from *agarazo*, which means to buy back from the slave market (of sin).

> ► *These are the ones who have not been defiled with women, for they have kept themselves chaste. These are the ones who follow the Lamb wherever He goes. These have been purchased from among men as first fruits to God and to the Lamb. And no lie was found in their mouth; they are blameless [Revelation 14:4,5].*

> Flee immorality. Every other sin that a man commits is outside the body, but the immoral man sins against his own body. Or do you not know that your body is a temple of the Holy Spirit who is in you, whom you have from God, and that you are not your own? For you have been bought with a price; therefore glorify God in your body [1 Corinthians 6:18-20].

Defiled is the Greek *moluno*, which is one of five Greek words that can be translated "defiled." *Moluno* is never used to refer to ceremonial uncleanness; it always refers to immorality or fornication. Therefore, these 144,000 have remained chaste throughout the Tribulation, have been totally devoted only to the Lord, and have refused to worship the antichrist. *First fruits* suggests they were the first converts to Christ during the Tribulation.

(b) Three holy angels warn of God's coming judgment. (This judgment is at Armageddon, which will occur at the very end of the Tribulation, further described in verses 15-20.)

> ▶ *And I saw another angel flying in midheaven, having an eternal gospel to preach to those who live on the earth, and to every nation and tribe and tongue and people [Revelation 14:6].*

Another is *allos*, which means another of the same kind. The last angel mentioned is back in Revelation 11:15, which was an holy angel. *Angel* is *angelos*, "messenger." *Midheaven* is probably in the midst of the atmosphere over the earth. God is always faithful to warn people of coming judgment.

An eternal gospel poses a small theological problem in that angels have never been commissioned to preach *the gospel* to the lost. God has always used people. However, notice that *eternal gospel* does not have the definite article. Also, "gospel" is *evangelion*, which simply means "good news" and does not have to refer to the Gospel of Jesus Christ. Context must always determine how a word is translated.

Preach is the verb *euangelizo*, which means to preach or proclaim good news. Furthermore, the message of the angel is given in verse 7, which is not *the* Gospel, but is the good news that God's judgment has come. God's judgment is good news to all believers still alive on earth.

Every nation and tribe and tongue and people is found seven times in the Book of the Revelation. The Gospel of Jesus Christ has by then been preached around the world by the 144,000.

> ▶ *(A)nd he said with a loud voice, "Fear God, and give Him glory, because the hour of His judgment has come; worship Him who made the heaven and the earth and sea and springs of waters" [Revelation 14:7].*

Fear God, and give Him glory ... and *worship Him* are in stark contrast to what most of the people on earth have been doing, namely, fearing and worshipping the beast. There may yet be a few people on

earth who have not received the mark of the beast and could trust Christ
as their Savior.

Judgment is from *krino*, which means to separate, to choose, to
determine, to pronounce judgment. God is about to separate everyone
in the world between those who trust in Him and those who don't. *Who
made the heaven and the earth and sea and springs of waters* is a
common reference to the creatorship of God. Such creatorship should
solicit gratitude and worship from His creatures. All of God's creation
has touched His creatures. Satan and the antichrist have created
nothing.

> ► *And another angel, a second one, followed, saying,
> "Fallen, fallen is Babylon the great, she who has made
> all the nations drink of the wine of the passion of her
> immorality" [Revelation 14:8].*

Another is *allos*, and so for every angel in this passage. *Fallen* is
repeated for emphasis. *Babylon the great* in Scripture either refers to a
literal city, a false religious system, or an evil political system. Both
Isaiah's and Jeremiah's prophecies state that the literal city of Babylon
is never to be rebuilt. Therefore, if this refers to a literal city, it is being
applied to a modern city that is wicked as Babylon was. The name
"Babylon the great" occurs again in Revelation 17:5 where it refers to
the false religious system that the beast uses to rise to world power,
then destroys her. Perhaps the best interpretation of Revelation 14:8 is
that it symbolizes the false religious system. However, such a system
would have a center (a city); in Revelation 18:2 the phrase, "Babylon
the great" is repeated, and does refer to a city. If the "seven mountains"
of Revelation 17:9 refer to the city of Rome, then Rome will be the
"Babylon the great" of the Book of Revelation. The "fallen," then, is
both the false religious system and the city in which it dwells. In fact,
the description given here, *she who has made*, is the same description
in Revelation 18:3.

> ► *Then another angel, a third one, followed them,
> saying with a loud voice, "If anyone worships the beast
> and his image, and receives a mark upon his forehead
> or on his hand, he also will drink of the wine of the
> wrath of God, which is mixed in full strength in the cup*

> *of His anger; and he will be tormented with fire and brimstone in the presence of the holy angels and in the presence of the Lamb. And the smoke of their torment goes up forever and ever; they have no rest day and night, those who worship the beast and his image, and whoever receives the mark of his name"[Revelation 14:9-11].*

Verses 9-11 answer the questions: *who? what? where? how long? what will it be like?* and *who?* The question *who?* occurs twice for emphasis. *Who?* is "anyone that **worships the beast and his image, and receives a mark on his forehead or upon his hand** (see Revelation 13:16-17, page 148).

What? is present judgment, namely, to **drink of the wine of the wrath of God.** This will come in the form of the Bowl Judgments just days prior to the end of the Tribulation (see Revelation 15:7 and 16:1-2). **He will be tormented with fire and brimstone** is future judgment. The *where?* is **in the presence of the holy angels and in the presence of the Lamb.** *How long?* is *forever and ever!* This is *eis aionas aionon,* a very strong Greek phrase to describe eternity (see Revelation 20:10, page 206).

What will it be like? is **they have no rest day and night.** *Who?* is answered again for emphasis, namely, **those who worship the beast and his image, and whoever receives the mark of his name.** Anyone who thinks that God will not punish Christ rejectors in the Lake of Fire forever must deal with this and other clear passages of Scripture. Their place of torment will be the Lake of Fire, or Hell (see Revelation 19:20).

Jesus referred to "hell" twelve times in the New Testament; eleven of those He used the Greek word, *gehenna.* He also used the word "fire" 19 times in the New Testament; in twelve of these 19 He was referring to the fire of hell (See also footnote 16, page 108).

> ► *Here is the perseverance of the saints who keep the commandments of God and their faith in Jesus [Revelation 14:12].*

Saints is *hagioi,* and means "set apart ones" (for holy purposes). Believers are "saints" by position, but not always in practice. Notice the relationship here between salvation and works: first, they are saints because they trust in Christ as their Savior; second, they *keep the commandments of God and their faith in Jesus.* They are saved first, then the works come. The total absence of works suggests the absence of salvation.

> But someone may well say, "you have faith and I have works; show me your faith without the works, and I will show you my faith by my works." You believe that God is one. You do well; the demons also believe, and shudder. But are you willing to recognize, you foolish fellow, that faith without works is useless? [James 2:18-20].

See also Luke 10:25-37.

> ► *And I heard a voice from heaven, saying, "Write, 'Blessed are the dead who die in the Lord from now on!' " "Yes," says the Spirit, "so that they may rest from their labors, for their deeds follow with them" [Revelation 14:13].*

The *voice* in Revelation 10:4 said "do not write," but here it says, *Write. Blessed* is *makarios,* which means to be supernaturally blessed, to be blessed of God. Notice that here the blessing is to *die in the Lord.* These "blessed ones" will be killed by the antichrist. Then, *they may rest,* but the Christ rejectors "have no rest," verse 11. *Their deeds follow with them* (the believers) in rewards.

> For no man can lay a foundation other than the one which is laid, which is Jesus Christ. Now if any man builds on the foundation with gold, silver, precious stones, wood, hay, straw, each man's work will become evident; for the day will show it because it is to be revealed with fire, and the fire itself will test the quality of each man's work. If any man's work which he has built on remains, he will *receive a reward.* If any man's work is burned up, he will suffer loss; but

he himself will be saved, yet so as through fire [1 Corinthians 3:11-15].

(c) The Son of Man prepares to execute God's judgment.

> ► *Then I looked, and behold, a white cloud, and sitting on the cloud was one like a son of man, having a golden crown on His head and a sharp sickle in His hand [Revelation 14:14].*

A white cloud is how Jesus went into heaven and will return in like manner.

> They also said, "Men of Galilee, why do you stand looking into the sky? This Jesus, who has been taken up from you into heaven, will come in just the same way as you have watched Him go into heaven" [Acts 1:11].

Son of man is a common title for Jesus Christ, an Old Testament title for the Messiah, which stresses his humanity. *A golden crown* will stress his Deity. "Crown" here is *stephanos*, the earned crown, which Jesus earned by His obedience to His Father.

The *sharp sickle* stresses His authority. The antichrist was human, but not Deity, and his authority came from Satan (Revelation 13:4). Jesus gets His authority from God.

> And Jesus came up and spoke to them, saying, "All authority has been given to Me in heaven and on earth" [Matthew 28:18].

> For not even the Father judges anyone, but He has given all judgment to the Son [John 5:22].

(d) Three holy angels bring God's judgment.

> ► *And another angel came out of the temple, crying out with a loud voice to Him who sat upon the cloud, "Put in your sickle and reap, for the hour to reap has come,*

because the harvest of the earth is ripe." Then He who
sat on the cloud swung His sickle over the earth, and
the earth was reaped [Revelation 14:15,16].

This next angel comes *out of the temple*; so while it may seem strange
that he is telling Jesus to *put in your sickle*, the angel is bringing the
message from God the Father, because angels are "messengers." Here
John is describing the authority of Jesus to bring judgment.

For not even the Father judges anyone, but He has
given all judgment to the Son .... and He gave Him
authority to execute judgment, because He is the Son
of Man [John 5:22, 27].

The harvest of the earth is the "end of the age."

(A)nd the enemy who sowed them is the devil, and the
harvest is the *end of the age*; and the reapers are angels
[Matthew 13:39].

Ripe is the Greek word *eksarantha*, which means to become dry, or
withered. The word "ripe" in verse 18 is *akmasan*, which means to be
fully ripe. This contrast differentiates between the symbolic swinging of
the sickle by Christ in verse 16 because He sees that the earth is "dry
and withered;" it is pitiful and ready for judgment. Then, in verses
17-20 comes the actual judgment carried out by the angel.

▶ *And another angel came out of the temple which is in*
heaven, and he also had a sharp sickle [Revelation
14:17].

This angel comes *out of the temple* with God's power and authority.

▶ *Then another angel, the one who has power over*
fire, came out from the altar; and he called with a loud
voice to him who had the sharp sickle, saying, "put in
your sharp sickle and gather the clusters from the vine
of the earth, because her grapes are ripe"[Revelation
14:18].

This final angel comes *out from the altar*, which is the source of God's judgment, and he is the one who commands the angel with the sickle. *The clusters* are people who are like plump clusters of grapes ready for the wine press. As grapes are smashed and their juice or "blood" runs out, so will the literal blood of these Christ-rejectors.

> ▶ *So the angel swung his sickle to the earth and gathered the clusters from the vine of the earth, and threw them into the great wine press of the wrath of God [Revelation 14:19].*

Swung and *threw* is the same word, *ballo*. *Great wine press* is symbolic of the wrath of God.

> ▶ *And the wine press was trodden outside the city, and blood came out from the wine press, up to the horses' bridles, for a distance of two hundred miles [Revelation 14:20].*

The city is Jerusalem. Since the blood will run as deep as horses' bridles in places for two hundred miles, it will extend beyond Israel's borders.

c. God prepares to pour out the Bowl Judgments, Revelation 15:1-8.

Chapter 15 now resumes the chronological sequence of God's judgments. Chapters 8-9 described the Trumpet Judgments, and Chapters 10-14 were a large parenthesis, or "flashback," which added detail as to what was happening during those judgments. Chapters 15 and 16 will now advance the series of events by preparing us for and describing the Bowl Judgments, the last of God's judgments upon the satanic world system.

(1) John saw the sign for the completion of God's wrath.

> ▶ *Then I saw another sign in heaven, great and marvelous, seven angels who had seven plagues, which are the last, because in them the wrath of God is finished [Revelation 15:1].*

Another is "allos," which means another of the same kind. The other signs that John saw were last described in Revelation 12:1 and 3, which also were signs "in heaven." A *sign* is a "semeion," which is an attesting miracle. It is something that God gives to confirm that *He* is the one behind the events. *Great and marvelous* occur together like this in Scripture only here and in verse 3.

Plagues is *plagas*, which means a blow, a smiting. The verb *plasso* means to strike, to smite, to wound, to blast. The words *the last* occur at the end of the "plagues" in the Greek text, correctly placed in the NASV for the sake of emphasis.

Wrath is *thumos*, which emphasizes the attitude or emotion of the person. It can translate as "anger" or "rage." *Is finished* is an aorist passive denoting completed action, from the verb *teleo*, meaning to complete, to conclude, to fulfill. It's the same root which gives *tetelestai* from John 19:30, where Jesus said from the cross, "It is finished!"

(2) The sign was a song about God and His Word.

> ► *And I saw something like a sea of glass mixed with fire, and those who had been victorious over the beast and his image and the number of his name, standing on the sea of glass, holding harps of God [Revelation 15:2].*

Something like is John's way of telling us that he is doing the best he can to describe what he is seeing, using all the terms he can. The *sea of glass* is the brazen laver in front of the Temple in heaven. It is filled with water that is so still that it looks like *glass*; it is so still because the blood of Christ has purified the saints and they have no need of washing. It is *mixed with fire*, which is the symbol of judgment, because the martyrs of the Tribulation are praying for God's revenge (Revelation 6:9-11). They are further described as *those who had been victorious over the beast and his image and the number of his name*.

These are unmistakably tribulation saints whom God sees as victorious because they have refused to give in to the satanic world system (see Revelation 14:13 and 20:4-6 for their rewards). They are *standing on the sea of glass*, which is a miracle itself. *Harps* is the *kitharas*, a ten-stringed instrument with two symmetrical arms and a connecting arm at the top which holds the strings. It is an instrument of worship.

> ► *And they sang the song of Moses, the bond-servant of God, and the song of the Lamb, saying, "Great and marvelous are Your works, O Lord God, the Almighty; Righteous and true are Your ways, King of the nations! Who will not fear, O Lord, and glorify Your name? For You alone are holy; For all the nations will come and worship before You, for Your righteous acts have been revealed" [Revelation 15:3, 4].*

They sang is *adousin*, which is present indicative, "they sing" or "they are singing," suggesting an ongoing action.

Bond-servant is *doulos*, a willing servant. *Lamb* suggests sacrifice and redemption. Moses and Christ bring the Old and New Testaments together.

> For the Law was given through Moses; grace and truth were realized through Jesus Christ [John 1:17].

The song of Moses and *the song of the Lamb* both have the definite article that suggests they are actually singing two songs. "The song of Moses" has two versions: one in Exodus 15 and one in Deuteronomy 32, both of which stress the faithfulness of God to Israel. This song is appropriate because Satan has been trying during the Tribulation to annihilate the nation of Israel. *The song of the Lamb* is probably a version of Revelation 5:8-14 (see also Revelation 7:10 that refers to a song by the martyred saints).

Are, which appears twice in this part of verse three, does not occur in the Greek text, but is an *elipsis*, or missing word that often occurs in Greek and must be supplied in English. Sometimes the *elipsis* is used to stress the act itself, or to stress both the past and future acts, as here. The song will describe some seven attributes of God:

● His omnipotence with *O Lord God, the Almighty*

- His absolute righteousness with *Righteous ... are your ways*

- His veracity with *True are your ways*

- His sovereignty with *King of the nations*

- His holiness and purity with *For you alone are holy*

- His worthiness to be worshipped with *all the nations will come and worship before you.*

Not is actually *ou ma*, a double negative that we cannot translate into English. The double negative stresses the negative aspect of the question (see Philippians 2:5-11). *Nations* is *ethnos*, which gives our English word "ethnic."

> All nations whom You have made shall come and worship before You, O Lord, and they shall glorify Your name [Psalm 86:9].

See also Zechariah 14:16-21.

Have been revealed is an aorist passive, a completed action, from *phaneroo*, which means to bring to light.

(3) John saw the seven angels receive the last seven plagues of God.

> ▶ *After these things I looked, and the temple of the tabernacle of testimony in heaven was opened [Revelation 15:5].*

After these things I looked is a way John introduces all new material - something he has never seen before. *Temple* is *naos*, which means "shrine," or the Holy of Holies inside the *tabernacle*. *Testimony* is *marturion*, which is the Ark of the Covenant containing the tablets of the Law of God. It was *opened* (Revelation 11:19), to let out the seven angels who have now received instructions from God to carry out His final judgments. Judgment is immediate (Revelation 14:15-17).

> ▶ *(A)nd the seven angels who had the seven plagues came out of the temple, clothed in linen, clean and bright, and girded around their chests with golden sashes [Revelation 15:6].*

Linen, clean and bright here represents the righteousness of God. It is God's righteousness that is the basis of all His judgment. He must deal with sin. **Golden sashes** show these are holy angels, representing God and His right to be worshipped and glorified.

> ▶ *Then one of the four living creatures gave to the seven angels seven golden bowls full of the wrath of God, who lives forever and ever [Revelation 15:7].*

For **four living creatures** see Revelation 4:6, page 78. **Bowl(s)** is *phialas*, which are **full** and are easily poured out. **Golden** again represents Deity. **Wrath** is *thumos* as in verse 1; it will demonstrate God's supremacy over Satan and his fallen angels. **Who lives forever and ever** describes the attribute of God as being *eternal*.

> ▶ *And the temple was filled with smoke from the glory of God and from His power; and no one was able to enter the temple until the seven plagues of the seven angels were finished [Revelation 15:8].*

Filled with smoke is like Exodus 19:18 when God came down upon Mt. Sinai, or Exodus 40:34-35 when God came into the tabernacle. **No one was able to enter the temple**, not even the holy angels.

> Now Mount Sinai was all in smoke because the LORD descended upon it in fire; and its smoke ascended like the smoke of a furnace, and the whole mountain quaked violently [Exodus 19:18].

Until the seven plagues ... were finished introduces Chapter 16.

d. The Seven Bowl Judgments and the redemption of the earth, Revelation 16:1-21.

162

While Chapter 15 was an introduction to God's Bowl Judgments, Chapter 16 records the actual outpouring of these bowls in God's final judgment of the satanic world system.[17]

(1) The first bowl attacks the worshippers of the beast.

> ► *Then I heard a loud voice from the temple, saying to the seven angels, "Go and pour out on the earth the seven bowls of the wrath of God" [Revelation 16:1].*

Loud is *megalas*, which appears nine times in this chapter. It is translated "loud" in verse 17, but "fierce" in verse 9, "great" in verses 12, 14, 18 and 19, and "extremely severe" in verse 21.

The **voice** came **from the temple** because in Revelation 15:8 no one could enter the temple until the plagues were finished.

Wrath is *thumos* as in Revelation 15:1, which stresses the attitude of the person, his anger, his rage. But, in verse 19, John uses the same word *thumos*, translated "fierce" with the word *orga*, which there translates as "wrath." **On the earth** as in verse 2 indicates a universal judgment upon the whole earth. While the Trumpet Judgments of Chapters 8 and 9 are very similar to the Bowl Judgments, they were deliberately limited to give mankind a chance to repent. Unfortunately, man by and large does not repent (see Revelation 16:9).

> ► *So the first angel went and poured out his bowl on the earth; and it became a loathsome and malignant sore on the people who had the mark of the beast and who worshipped his image [Revelation 16:2].*

Loathsome is *kakos*, which means evil or bad. **Malignant** is *ponaros*, which means bad, unsound, evil, wicked. **Sore** is *helkos*, which means an ulcer, a sore, a boil, a wound. The Septuagint, the Greek translation of the Old Testament, uses this word to translate the "boils" on the

---

[17] One must remember that as the judgment of God is carefully considered in these verses, that God is still a kind, merciful, loving God. But His pleas and warnings have gone unheeded by unregenerate, Christ-rejecting persons. God's sovereignty over His creation and His absolute righteousness now demands judgment in preparation for Christ's rule upon the earth.

Egyptians in Exodus 9:8-12. As those boils were only upon the Egyptians, so here it will be only upon *the people who had the mark of the beast.* The definite article appears here and is translated. Then, in verses 8, 9, and 21, the definite article is found again, but untranslated. It is not understood why this is not translated into English. It seems that these Bowl Judgments are directed specifically toward these Christ-rejectors, the unregenerate, God-blaspheming persons who deserve God's worst punishment upon them. Some of these Bowl Judgments are directed to God's creation, but even those are designed to punish the beast-worshippers.

(2) The second bowl attacks the sea and everything in it.

> ► *The second angel poured out his bowl into the sea, and it became blood like that of a dead man; and every living thing in the sea died [Revelation 16:3].*

Blood like that of a dead man is coagulated and lifeless. This judgment is obviously universal because *every living thing in the sea died.*

(3) The third bowl attacks all fresh water.

> ► *Then the third angel poured out his bowl into the rivers and springs of waters; and they became blood [Revelation 16:4].*

The rivers and the springs of waters are all the fresh waters of the earth. Without this fresh water to drink, man can only survive a few days. These, too, *became blood,* like the Nile River (see Exodus 7:20).

> ► *And I heard the angel of the waters saying, "Righteous are You, who are and who were, O Holy One, because You judged these things [Revelation 16:5].*

The angel of the waters is evidently a holy angel who has the special ministry over fresh water of the earth. The angel gives the attributes of God as the legal basis for His judgments: His absolute righteousness, His eternality, and His holiness (compare Revelation 15:3-4).

> ► *(F)or they poured out the blood of saints and prophets, and You have given them blood to drink. They deserve it [Revelation 16:6].*

They refers all the way back to its antecedent in verse 2, "the men who had the mark of the beast." Such pouring **out the blood of saints** was warned by Jesus in Matthew 24:20-22.

They deserve it again refers to those Christ-rejectors.

> ► *And I heard the altar saying, "Yes, O Lord God, the Almighty, true and righteous are Your judgments" [Revelation 16:7].*

The altar saying means that John heard a voice from the altar, the place of judgment.

(4) The fourth bowl intensifies the sun.

> ► *The fourth angel poured out his bowl upon the sun, and it was given to it to scorch men with fire [Revelation 16:8].*

Men is actually "the men" in the Greek text. See notes on verse 2, pages 159-160.

> ► *Men were scorched with fierce heat; and they blasphemed the name of God who has the power over these plagues, and they did not repent so as to give Him glory [Revelation 16:9].*

Blasphemed is from *blasphiami*, which means calumny, a false accusation of a crime or offense. These accusations are purposed to slander someone's good name, in this case God's name.

Plagues is the same word *plagas*, found back in Revelation 15:1; the verb means to strike, blast, wound. **They did not repent** is from *metanoeo*, which means to change the mind, to do an about-face, to turn around. They refused to turn from their wicked ways of following the beast and refused to follow Christ. **Glory** is recognition of God's true greatness in His power, sovereignty and grace. Glory is the sum of all God's attributes.

(5) The fifth bowl darkens the sun.

> ▶ *Then the fifth angel poured out his bowl on the throne of the beast, and his kingdom became darkened; and they gnawed their tongues because of pain [Revelation 16:10].*

The throne of the beast is probably in political Babylon described in Chapter 18. *The beast* is the first beast of Revelation 13:1-10. *Darkened* is like what God did to Egypt in Exodus 10:21-23 because one of their gods was "Ra," the sun god. *Because of pain* is from the sores described in verse 2.

> ▶ *(A)nd they blasphemed the God of heaven because of their pains and their sores; and they did not repent of their deeds [Revelation 16:11].*

Their deeds reveal their unrepentant hearts.

(6) The sixth bowl dries up the Euphrates River.

> ▶ *The sixth angel poured out his bowl on the great river, the Euphrates; and its water was dried up, so that the way would be prepared for the kings from the east [Revelation 16:12].*

The great river, the Euphrates has always been a significant boundary throughout history. It has always been the dividing line between East and West. Ancient Rome had the Euphrates as its eastern boundary. This river separates the East from the Middle East. For *dried up*, Isaiah and Zechariah both speak of this same event.

> And the LORD will utterly destroy the tongue of the Sea of Egypt; and He will wave His hand over the River with His scorching wind; and He will strike it into seven streams and make men walk over dry-shod....And they will pass through the sea of distress

and He will strike the waves in the sea, so that all the depths of the Nile (river, KJV) will dry up; and the pride of Assyria will be brought down and the scepter of Egypt will depart [Isaiah 11:15; Zechariah 10:11].

The kings from the east will invade Israel to challenge the world government of the antichrist. Daniel 11 speaks of the "king of the North" and the "king of the South," but here it says "kings," a plural, perhaps a confederacy of China, Japan and India. *East* is in relation to Jerusalem.

> ▶ *And I saw coming out of the mouth of the dragon and out of the mouth of the beast and out of the mouth of the false prophet, three unclean spirits like frogs [Revelation 16:13].*

So, the source of authority opposing God is the "unholy trinity:" the dragon is Satan himself, imitating God; the beast is the antichrist, imitating Christ; and the false prophet imitates the Holy Spirit by using signs and wonders to get people to worship the beast.

> ▶ *(F)or they are spirits of demons, performing signs, which go out to the kings of the whole world, to gather them together for the war of the great day of God, the Almighty [Revelation 16:14].*

Demons is *daimonion*, which are evil, fallen angels. *Signs* is *semeion*, an attesting miracle, the same as Revelation 15:1 (see Revelation 13:11-15). *War* is *polemos*, not *macha*, which means a battle (see also Daniel 11:40-45).

> ▶ *("Behold, I am coming like a thief. Blessed is the one who stays awake and keeps his clothes, so that he will not walk around naked and men will not see his shame") [Revelation 16:15].*

A thief comes quickly and with harm to whomever is not watching. Here is a clear reference to the Second Advent of Christ as a coming thief.

But be sure of this, that *if the head of the house had
known* at what hour the thief was coming, he would not
have allowed his house to be broken into [Luke 12:39].

Keeps his clothes is a reference to the behavior of believers (see
Revelation 3:4).

> ► *And they gathered them together to the place which
> in Hebrew is called Har-Magedon [Revelation 16:16].*

Har-Magedon means the "Hill of Megiddo," which is on the southern
edge of the Valley of Jezreel, the center of what will be the last great
battle of the world. The valley of Jezreel is in the form of an inverted
triangle, 15 by 15 by 20 miles, with the 20 miles at the top. Nazareth
overlooks this great valley on the east, and Mt. Carmel on the west. The
"Hill of Megiddo" is at the southernmost point of the triangle.

(7) The seventh bowl destroys the surface of the earth.

> ► *Then the seventh angel poured out his bowl upon the
> air, and a loud voice came out of the temple from the
> throne, saying, "It is done" [Revelation 16:17].*

It is done is *gegonen* not *tetelestai* as in Revelation 15:1. The authority
came again *from the throne* (not the throne of antichrist).

> ► *And there were flashes of lightning and sounds and
> peals of thunder; and there was a great earthquake,
> such as there had not been since man came to be upon
> the earth, so great an earthquake was it, and so mighty
> [Revelation 16:18].*

Lightning ... thunder ... earthquake also occurred at the end of the
Seal Judgments, Revelation 8:5, and the Trumpet Judgments,
Revelation 11:19.

> ► *The great city was split into three parts, and the
> cities of the nations fell. Babylon the great was
> remembered before God, to give her the cup of the
> wine of His fierce wrath [Revelation 16:19].*

The great city may refer to Jerusalem or perhaps to Babylon.

For **cup**,

> For a *cup* is in the hand of the LORD, and the wine foams; it is well mixed, and He pours out of this; surely all the wicked of the earth must drain and drink down its dregs [Psalm 75:8].

> ▶ *And every island fled away, and the mountains were not found. And huge hailstones, about one hundred pounds each, came down from heaven upon men; and men blasphemed God because of the plague of the hail, because its plague was extremely severe [Revelation 16:20, 21].*

How can anyone say that these verses have already been fulfilled? There is nothing recorded in the histories of the world's nations that suggest such catastrophe has occurred. Weather records exist of hailstones the size of softballs, but there is no record of any that have weighed 100 pounds.

Men is actually "the men" in the Greek text which strongly suggests that all surviving believers (there will be some, see Matthew 25:34-40) will be spared from these terrible plagues.

e. Third "flashback," the holy angels give John more detail of the Tribulation, Revelation 17-18.

(1) In the first half of the Tribulation, ecclesiastical Babylon is destroyed by the antichrist, Revelation 17:1-18.

(a) John sees the vision of Ecclesiastical Babylon.

Ecclesiastical comes from the Greek word *ecclasia*, which means "called out ones," and is usually translated "church" in the New Testament. In Chapter 17 the English word is used to refer to a world-wide church. It is *not* the Universal Church of Jesus Christ; *The Church* has already been raptured.

This world-wide "church" is an apostate church, a false church, a combination of all false religions of the world. The description of this Babylon is obviously an organized religion that is destroyed by another Babylon described in Chapter 18, which is obviously a political system. The word "Babylon" is used for both because in Biblical history (see Genesis 10:8-10 and 11:1-9), the origin of rebellion against God was both religious and political. During the Tribulation, it will be religious and political again.

[1] The apostate church leads the whole world astray.

> ► *Then one of the seven angels who had the seven bowls came and spoke with me, saying, "Come here, I will show you the judgment of the great harlot who sits on many waters" [Revelation 17:1].*

Chapter 17 begins another parenthesis or "flashback" to give more details of the Tribulation. In this case, the angel relates events from the first of the Tribulation after the Holy Spirit, the *Restrainer*, is removed at the Rapture of the Church.

> For the mystery of lawlessness is already at work; only he who now restrains will do so now until he is taken out of the way [2 Thessalonians 2:7].

Harlot is *porna*, which gives our English word "pornography." In noun form, as here, it is appropriately translated "harlot" or "prostitute." The Nation Israel was said "to play the harlot" whenever she left the true God for a false god.

> For their mother has *played the harlot*; she who conceived them has acted shamefully. For she said, "I will go after my lovers, who give me my bread and my water, my wool and my flax, my oil and my drink .... But you trusted in your beauty and *played the harlot* because of your fame, and you poured out your harlotries on every passer-by who might be willing .... and they *played the harlot* in Egypt. They *played the harlot* in their youth; there their breasts were pressed

and there their virgin bosom was handled [Hosea 2:5; Ezekiel 16:15, 23:3].

Sits gives the idea of control. *Many waters* is identified in verse 15 as "peoples and multitudes and nations and tongues."

> ▶ *(W)ith whom the kings of the earth committed acts of immorality, and those who dwell on the earth were made drunk with the wine of her immorality [Revelation 17:2].*

Committed acts of immorality is the verb *porneuo*, which is the same root as "harlot." Therefore, the apostate church *and* the kings of the earth have left the true God for false gods. This is *the joining of the church and state,* when laws *will* be passed to control religion. These laws will make it illegal to worship and serve Jesus Christ, and it will be worldwide.

Made drunk with the wine of her immorality describes the excesses of false religion, just like a person getting drunk.

[2] The apostate church uses the antichrist to gain this world-wide power.

> ▶ *And he carried me away in the Spirit into a wilderness; and I saw a woman sitting on a scarlet beast, full of blasphemous names, having seven heads and ten horns [Revelation 17:3].*

For *in the Spirit,* see pages 22 and 73. The *wilderness* translated in the KJV does not have the article in the Greek, so the NASV correctly translates "a wilderness."

A woman was used to represent the nation Israel back in Revelation 12:1. Here "a woman" is used to represent this apostate church, now *sitting* or dominating and controlling *a scarlet beast,* who is the antichrist of Revelation 13:1. Obviously, this "harlot" is separate from the "beast." The *seven heads* are seven kings left after the antichrist takes over the ten nations or kingdoms that are represented by the *ten horns.*

> ► *The woman was clothed in purple and scarlet, and adorned with gold and precious stones and pearls, having in her hand a gold cup full of abominations and of the unclean things of her immorality [Revelation 17:4].*

Purple and scarlet were the colors worn by royalty, so she sees herself as a ruler. *Gold and precious stones and pearls* are evidence of her wealth, but also a false spirituality. The *gold cup* is *full* because the Restrainer, the Holy Spirit has been withdrawn.

> ► *(A)nd on her forehead a name was written, a mystery, "BABYLON THE GREAT, THE MOTHER OF HARLOTS AND OF THE ABOMINATIONS OF THE EARTH" [Revelation 17:5].*

The *Babylon* of Chapter 17 is distinct and different from the Babylon of Chapter 18. *Upon her forehead* was the same spot that Jesus sealed His bond-servants in Revelation 7:3. After the antichrist destroys the apostate church at the midpoint of the Tribulation, the false prophet will use his power and influence to place seals on the foreheads of those who follow the first beast (see Revelation 13:16-18, pages 148-149).

Mystery is in small letters in the NASV, taken to be an introduction to, but not part of, the title. It means, "that which has not before been revealed."

Babylon, as a city, is the second most mentioned city in the Bible, second only to Jerusalem. Here, *Babylon the Great* is part of her title that stresses the religious trappings of ancient Babylon, but not the city itself; this comes in Chapter 18.

Mother of harlots and of the abominations of the earth shows that this apostate church spawns the world-wide rebellion against God in the Tribulation. "Abomination" is that word in Scripture that includes idolatry, which is an abomination to God.

[3] The apostate church will kill true believers in Christ.

> ▶ *And I saw the woman drunk with the blood of the saints, and with the blood of the witnesses of Jesus. When I saw her, I wondered greatly [Revelation 17:6].*

Drunk with the blood shows "the woman" has no tolerance for those who worship and serve Jesus Christ (compare this to Revelation 6:10; 7:14 and 16:6). **Wondered** is from *thaumazo*, which means to be "astonished."

(b) John hears the interpretation of the vision.

[1] The power of the apostate church is the antichrist.

> ▶ *And the angel said to me, "Why do you wonder? I will tell you the mystery of the woman and of the beast that carries her, which has the seven heads and the ten horns" [Revelation 17:7].*

Carries shows the power and ability behind the apostate church.

> ▶ *The beast that you saw was, and is not, and is about to come up out of the abyss and go to destruction. And those who dwell on the earth, whose name has not been written in the book of life from the foundation of the world, will wonder when they see the beast, that he was and is not and will come [Revelation 17:8].*

Was, and is not, and is about to occurs three times: twice in this verse and again in verse 11 in a slightly different form.

References to **the abyss** are found in Revelation 9:1, 2 and 11; 11:7; here; and in Revelation 20:1 and 3. Satan in Revelation 9:11 is said to have the power over the abyss; therefore, Satan gives his power to the beast, and the beast gives his power to the apostate church. **Destruction** is the ultimate end of the beast and Satan. *Apoleia* is the same word translated "perish" in John 3:16, and the same in Revelation 17:11.

> ▶ *Here is the mind which has wisdom. The seven heads are seven mountains on which the woman sits [Revelation 17:9].*

Seven mountains have been identified with Rome on coins and by poets from ancient times. This suggests that the world-wide apostate church could have its headquarters in Rome. Some have suggested that the antichrist might use Roman Catholicism as the religion that unites all world religions during the Tribulation.

> ► *(A)nd they are seven kings; five have fallen, one is, the other has not yet come; and when he comes, he must remain a little while [Revelation 17:10].*

This verse is difficult to interpret. Some take these seven kings to refer to Roman dynasties; other to the seven gentile world-dominating powers throughout history, namely: Egypt, Assyria, Babylon, Medo-Persia, Greece (the first five), then Rome (the *sixth*, during John's time), and the *seventh*, a revived Roman Empire under the antichrist. This would explain the **little while** of only seven years while the other powers ruled sometimes for centuries.

> ► *The beast which was and is not, is himself also an eighth and is one of the seven, and he goes to destruction [Revelation 17:11].*

The **eighth** is **one of the seven** because he heads the seventh, the gentile world-dominating power – the revived Roman Empire.

> ► *The ten horns which you saw are ten kings who have not yet received a kingdom, but they receive authority as kings with the beast for one hour [Revelation 17:12].*

One hour stresses purpose, not length of time. Compare the "hour" in Luke 22:53.

> While I was with you daily in the temple, you did not lay hands on Me; but this *hour* and the power of darkness are yours [Luke 22:53].

[2] The antichrist destroys the apostate church.

> ► *These have one purpose, and they give their power and authority to the beast. These will wage war against the Lamb, and the Lamb will overcome them, because He is Lord of lords and King of kings, and those who are with Him are the called chosen and faithful. And he said to me, "The waters which you saw where the harlot sits, are peoples and multitudes and nations and tongues" [Revelation 17:13-15].*

Once the apostate church gives its power to the antichrist at the mid-point of the Tribulation, the antichrist will destroy that church. Its "purpose" will have then been fulfilled.

> ► *And the ten horns which you saw, and the beast, these will hate the harlot and will make her desolate and naked, and will eat her flesh and will burn her up with fire. For God has put it in their hearts to execute His purpose by having a common purpose, and by giving their kingdom to the beast, until the words of God will be fulfilled [Revelation 17:16,17].*

This morbid destruction of the apostate church is executed so that Satan, who indwells the antichrist, can be worshipped directly, a goal that Satan has always had (see Matthew 4:8, 9). The religious leaders will be slaughtered! This verse shows the sovereignty of God again working behind the scenes of human history, allowing one evil faction to kill off another.

> ► *The woman whom you saw is the great city, which reigns over the kings of the earth [Revelation 17:18].*

The great city is probably Rome, and the city that God destroys in Chapter 18 will probably be a rebuilt Babylon in modern day Iraq.

(2) In the second half of the Tribulation, political Babylon is destroyed by God, Revelation 18:1-24.

While there are similarities between "Babylon the Great" in Chapter 17 and "Babylon the Great" in Chapter 18, there are notable differences that show us that these are two different Babylons. For example, the

Babylon of Chapter 17 is religious (called a harlot and spiritually immoral in Revelation 17:1-5), while the Babylon of Chapter 18 is economic (the merchants of Revelation 18:3). Also, the Babylon of Chapter 17 is destroyed by the beast, Revelation 17:16, while the Babylon of Chapter 18 is destroyed by the plagues of God, Revelation 18:8. Their similarities are the result of the apostate church, the religious Babylon of Chapter 17, assimilating the characteristics of the satanic world system, the political Babylon, of Chapter 18.

(a) John sees the vision of the political Babylon.

> ▶ *After these things I saw another angel coming down from heaven, having great authority, and the earth was illumined with his glory [Revelation 18:1].*

After these things denotes a continuation of the sequence, as in Revelation 4:1 and 7:9. This further supports the conclusion that the Babylons of Chapter 17 and 18 are different Babylons. *Another* is *allos*, meaning "another of the same kind," as the seven angels of Revelation 17:1, which had authority from God, Revelation 15:6. *From heaven* also indicates a holy angel with power from God because the Devil and his angels had been cast out in Revelation 12:7-9. *His glory* is not his own, but glory derived from being in the unveiled presence of God.

> ... I say to you that their angels in heaven continually see the face of My Father who is in heaven .... and His appearance was *like lightning*, and His clothing as *white as snow* [Matthew 18:10b; 28:3 (see also Exodus 34:29-35)].

> ▶ *And he cried out with a mighty voice, saying, "Fallen, fallen is Babylon the great! She has become a dwelling place of demons and a prison of every unclean spirit, and a prison of every unclean and hateful bird" [Revelation 18:2].*

Fallen is repeated for emphasis; both are aorist tense denoting completed action. The angel is revealing to John what must come to pass.

Babylon the great is either the literal city of Babylon rebuilt, or is a figurative reference as was the religious Babylon of Chapter 17. Isaiah 13 and Jeremiah 50 both predict that the literal city of Babylon would be destroyed, never to be rebuilt; but the context of Isaiah 13 refers to "The Day of the Lord," a reference to the Tribulation (see footnote 2, page 8).

Therefore, those passages have not yet been totally fulfilled. The destruction of the ancient city of Babylon was gradual, not "in one day" as it says in verse 10. Interestingly, Babylon is called *a dwelling place of demons,* and ancient Babylon is located on the Euphrates, referred to in Revelation 9:14 as the place of four terrible demons. The same applies to the phrase *a prison of every unclean spirit.*

Prison is *phulaka,* which means prison, hold, or cage.

> ▶ *For all the nations have drunk of the wine of the passion of her immorality, and the kings of the earth have committed acts of immorality with her, and the merchants of the earth have become rich by the wealth of her sensuality [Revelation 18:3].*

All the nations shows as it did in Chapter 17 that this political Babylon has become a world-wide power, the very thing that brings certain judgment from God.

Drunk of the wine ... acts of immorality appears very similar to Revelation 17:2, but the added feature of this Babylon is *the merchants of the earth have become rich by the wealth of her sensuality.* See also verses 11 and 15.

The nations have turned to the satanic world system instead of to God to find their satisfaction. They seek their fulfillment from Satan instead of the God who has created them. Such Christ-rejection is worthy of God's fiercest judgments.

(b) John hears the warning to God's people to get out of Babylon.

> ▶ *I heard another voice from heaven, saying, "Come out of her, my people, so that you will not participate*

in her sins and receive of her plagues" [Revelation 18:4].

Another is *allos*, another of the same kind. Compare this **voice** to the angel's voice in verse 2 - "a mighty voice." The message is *from heaven*, as was the angel in verse 1. The quote that begins here in verse 4 is not closed by the NASV translators until the end of verse 24.

Come out of her is reminiscent of God's call to Noah and his family to get into the ark, and to Lot and his family to get out of Sodom. *My people* shows that there are true believers around the world during the Tribulation, even in the city of Babylon. *That* introduces the purpose for the call ... *that you might not participate in her sins and receive of her plagues*, which will come from God (Revelation 16:17-21, the Bowl Judgments).

> ▶ *(F)or her sins have piled up as high as heaven, and God has remembered her iniquities [Revelation 18:5].*

Piled up is *kollao*, which means glued or welded together. It reminds us of how the Tower of Babel (see Genesis 11), was built to become the political and religious center of the world, but in rejection of God and His will for man. *God has remembered* shows that God does remember man's iniquity and does eventually bring judgment.

> Never take your own revenge, beloved, but leave room for the wrath of God, for it is written, "Vengeance is Mine, *I will repay*," says the Lord [Romans 12:19].

> ▶ *Pay her back even as she has paid, and give back to her double according to her deeds; in the cup which she has mixed, mix twice as much for her [Revelation 18:6].*

Pay back is *apodidomi*, which means to pay back, to repay a debt (see Revelation 6:9-11). *Give back double* does not mean that God is being unfair or unjust; it simply means that He is now showing *no mercy*. The term *mixed* is *kerannumi*, the same as in Revelation 14:10 describing God's wrath.

> ▶ *To the degree that she glorified herself and lived sensuously, to the same degree give her torment and mourning, for she says in her heart, "I sit as a queen and I am not a widow, and will never see mourning" [Revelation 18:7].*

She glorified herself is from *estraniasen*, meaning to be hardheaded, to be strong, to be head-strong. *Give her torment* is from *basanismon*, which means trial by torture.

> (T)he commander ordered him to be brought into the barracks, stating that he should be *examined by scourging* so that he might find out the reason why they were shouting against him that way [Acts 22:24].

What she says in her heart amounts to pure pride and playing God. *She says ... I will never see mourning* amounts to blasphemy, because she rejects God's will and right to rule over the earth.

> ▶ *For this reason in one day her plagues will come, pestilence and mourning and famine, and she will be burned up with fire; for the Lord God who judges her is strong [Revelation 18:8].*

In one day appears first in this sentence in the Greek text for emphasis. See also "one hour" in verses 10, 17 and 19. The *plagues* refer to the Bowl Judgments of Chapter 16; this Babylon is destroyed by God's plagues, not the antichrist, as was the Babylon in Revelation 17:16. It is interesting to compare the story of the rich fool in Luke 12:16-20 to the *pride* of this political Babylon who thinks she is invincible. Clearly, it is *the Lord God who judges her*.

(c) John hears the world mourning over the destruction of Babylon.

> ▶ *And the kings of the earth, who committed acts of immorality and lived sensuously with her, will weep and lament over her when they see the smoke of her burning [Revelation 18:9].*

The kings of the earth show more evidence of world-wide rebellion against God. This also stresses the political, as well as the economic, Babylon. The context of verses 11-16 defines *acts of immorality* as materialism lust, a form of idolatry.

> Therefore consider the members of your earthly body
> as dead to *immorality, impurity, passion, evil desire,*
> *and greed,* which amounts to idolatry [Colossians 3:5].

Weep is the Greek, *klaio*, which means to weep vocally, to wail. *Lament* is *kopto*, which means to beat the breast, in grief.

> ► *(S)tanding at a distance because of the fear of her*
> *torment, saying, "Woe, woe, the great city, Babylon,*
> *the strong city! For in one hour your judgment has*
> *come" [Revelation 18:10].*

Standing at a distance because of the fear of her torment proves the old saying that "there are no friends in jail." Wicked men flock together to share profits, but when retribution comes, they abandon each other instantly. *Woe* is *ouai*, which is used for warning, especially of impending doom, and especially when death is included (see Revelation 8:13).

One hour can be used to express purpose (Revelation 17:12), and brevity, (Revelation 18:17, 19). In Daniel 5, Babylon was captured, but not destroyed. Here, it is totally and suddenly destroyed.

> ► *And the merchants of the earth weep and mourn over*
> *her, because no one buys their cargoes any more*
> *[Revelation 18:11].*

Weep and mourn are both present participles of attendant circumstance. Obviously, the circumstance is Babylon's judgment in verse 10. The point is that the merchants are weeping and mourning over God's judgment of a Godless city. Compare verse 20, where "rejoicing" is much more appropriate.

Because no one buys their cargoes any more shows the totally selfish reasons for the weeping and mourning. This relationship was strictly for personal profit.

> ► *(C)argoes of gold and silver and precious stones and pearls and fine linen and purple and silk and scarlet, and every kind of citron wood and every article of ivory and every article made from very costly wood and bronze and iron and marble [Revelation 18:12].*

The description of goods in this verse suggests that the city of Babylon was still under construction. This helps to support the argument that ancient Babylon will be rebuilt. This also suggests it will be the headquarters of the one world government under the antichrist. The great wealth of the world will be pouring into this capital city, becoming the richest city of the world during the Tribulation.

> ► *(A)nd cinnamon and spice and incense and perfume and frankincense and wine and olive oil and fine flour and wheat and cattle and sheep, and cargoes of horses and chariots and slaves and human lives [Revelation 18:13].*

The first five items described in this verse could only be afforded by the wealthy during John's day. The people working for the antichrist during the Tribulation will become vastly wealthy. The next eleven things are very common things that will be found in great abundance in Babylon. Unfortunately, human slaves will be so common as to be considered with cattle and sheep.

Slaves is literally "bodies," which are unwilling slaves. **Human lives** is literally "souls of men," indicating a permanent slavery in which the slave has no hope of release. The Bible actually allows for slavery, but under strict guidelines, usually to work off a debt.

> ► *The fruit you long for has gone from you, and all things that were luxurious and splendid have passed away from you and men will no longer find them [Revelation 18:14].*

Long for is *epithumia*, which is a Greek word for a very strong desire; it is used in good and bad senses in the New Testament. It might here be translated "lusted for." Notice that they had lusted for "things" instead of God who has made all things. See Matthew 6:19-24 where Jesus warns of earthly treasure as opposed to heavenly treasure, which comes from faith and devotion and service to God.

> ► *The merchants of these things, who became rich from her, will stand at a distance because of the fear of her torment, weeping and mourning, saying, "Woe, woe, the great city, she who was clothed in fine linen and purple and scarlet, and adorned with gold and precious stones and pearls" [Revelation 18:15,16].*

Woe, woe is the second of three times this couplet appears in this chapter (see verses 10 and 19). *Was clothed* and *adorned* are both perfect passive participles. The perfect tense denotes past action with present, on-going results. Compare this to the aorist indicative passive verb in verse 17 - "has been laid waste" - which denotes a completed action and is the main verb for the two participles. The main verb there is *aramoo*, which means to lay waste, to bring to ruin, to make into a desolation. The prophecies of Isaiah 13 and Jeremiah 50 will then come to pass.

> ► *(F)or in one hour such great wealth has been laid waste! And every shipmaster and every passenger and sailor, and as many as make their living by the sea, stood at a distance [Revelation 18:17].*

Every shipmaster is each captain of the ships. The Euphrates River is navigable, and is the river on which ancient Babylon was built. Some Bible scholars see the rebuilt city as the one to fulfill all these prophecies. This is not a condition; however, to be met before the Church could be raptured. Babylon could be rebuilt *during* the tribulation period, after the rapture of the Church.

> ► *(A)nd were crying out as they saw the smoke of her burning, saying, "What city is like the great city?" [Revelation 18:18].*

The smoke of her burning could be the results of hail, fire and brimstone (as part of the seventh bowl, Revelation 16:17-21), or it could be the results of the huge earthquake (Revelation 16:18), during which the earth opens and swallows up Babylon, burning her completely up.

> ► *And they threw dust on their heads and were crying out, weeping and mourning, saying, "Woe, woe, the great city, in which all who had ships at sea became rich by her wealth, for in one hour she has been laid waste!" [Revelation 18:19].*

Weeping and mourning and *became rich by her wealth* shows that these are weeping only over their own losses, caring little about the loss of human life.

(d) John hears the call for heaven to rejoice over the destruction of Babylon.

> ► *Rejoice over her, O heaven, and you saints and apostles and prophets, because God has pronounced judgment for you against her [Revelation 18:20].*

Rejoice is *euphraino* in the present imperative passive. The imperative mood is the mood of command. It gives our English word "euphoric." We might translate this "be euphoric," "be elated." *O heaven* is everyone in heaven. Here, God has answered the prayers of the martyred saints, whose prayers were the Fifth Seal Judgment, Revelation 6:10.

You saints are the believers left on the earth; *apostles and prophets* are New Testament and Old Testament spokesmen for God. The Greek text presents this as four different groups, and the English word "you" has been supplied but the translators did not put it in italics. *For you* is genitive, not dative, which would be better translated "your judgment," to carry the idea that this is what the martyrs of God could do to Babylon, but the vengeance was carried out by God as He promised in Romans 12:19 in fulfillment of Revelation 6:9-11 (see verse 24).

> ► *Then a strong angel took up a stone like a great millstone and threw it into the sea, saying, "So will Babylon, the great city, be thrown down with violence, and will not be found any longer" [Revelation 18:21].*

The **great millstone** is a demonstration of total destruction and disappearance. *Any longer* appears seven times in various forms in verses 14, 21, and 24.

> ► *And the sound of harpists and musicians and flute-players and trumpeters will not be heard in you any longer; and no craftsman of any craft will be found in you any longer; and the sound of a mill will not be heard in you any longer; and the light of a lamp will not shine in you any longer; and the voice of the bridegroom and bride will not be heard in you any longer; for your merchants were the great men of the earth, because all the nations were deceived by your sorcery. And in her was found the blood of prophets and of saints and of all who have been slain on the earth [Revelation 18:22-24].*

Notice the ominous impression of *silence* and *darkness* in these verses. God's judgment upon this great city will be thorough, complete, and permanent.

C. The Second Coming of Christ, Revelation 19:1-21.

The entire Book of the Revelation has been an introduction to Chapter 19. The theme for the book is *Jesus Christ will rightfully rule on the earth*. This chapter tells us of the return of Christ to do just that.

1. Heaven dramatically announces the Second Advent of Christ, Revelation 19:1-10.[18]

a. The first "Hallelujah"

---

[18] The phrases, "First Advent" and "Second Advent" of Christ do not appear in the Old or New Testament. The departure of Christ after His resurrection is only inferred in the Old Testament.

> ▶ *After these things I heard something like a loud voice of a great multitude in heaven, saying, "Hallelujah! Salvation and glory and power belong to our God" [Revelation 19:1].*

After these things is the same phrase that John uses in Revelation 18:1 to continue a sequence of events; hence, the Second Advent of Christ will immediately follow the Bowl Judgments. If Jesus did not return immediately after the Bowl Judgments, everyone who survived the Tribulation would perish, including believers.

This chapter will be in stark contrast to Chapters 6-18, which contain the judgments of God. It will be a change from wickedness to righteousness, from judgment to grace. The greatest blessing the world can now receive is the physical return of Christ.

A loud voice is often used to designate something very important. *A great multitude in heaven* is not specifically identified, but probably includes all those of Revelation 18:20. *Hallelujah* is a Greek word transliterated from two Hebrew words: *hallel,* which means to praise, and *jah,* which is a shortened form of "Yahweh." It means "Praise Yahweh." It is found only four times in the New Testament; all four are right here in this passage. The Hebrew is imperative mood, the mood of command. *Salvation* is *sotaria,* which can be translated "deliverance," which here refers to Christ's deliverance of earth from the power and control of Satan (see Revelation 20:3).

Glory is *doksa,* which is the shining of God, the manifestation of His purity and morality, especially in judgment. *Power* is *dunamis,* and applies here specifically to God's power over Satan and his antichrist.

Our shows the personal nature of God, even in the midst of judgment.

> ▶ *Because His judgments are true and righteous; for He has judged the great harlot who was corrupting the earth with her immorality, and He has avenged the blood of His bond-servants on her [Revelation 19:2].*

Because is a reference to Psalm 19:9.

> The fear of the LORD is clean, enduring forever; the *judgments* of the LORD are *true*; they are *righteous* altogether [Psalm 19:9].

This explains why the actions of verse 1 are attributed to God: because of His attributes, His own personal characteristics are manifested in His deeds.

True is *alatheia*, which means intrinsic truth; God *is* truth.

> Jesus said to him, "I am the way, and *the truth*, and the life; no one comes to the Father but through Me" [John 14:6].

Righteous is *dikaios*, which means absolute righteousness; God *is* holy.

> (B)ecause it is written, "You shall be holy, for *I am holy*" [1 Peter 1:16].

Has judged is an aorist tense, completed action that was described in Chapter 17; **has avenged** is the same tense, because of her deeds (verse 17:b). So, God has righteously judged "the great harlot," or ecclesiastical Babylon, Chapter 17, and **avenged the blood** that was shed by the apostate church (see Romans 12:19).

Was corrupting is the imperfect tense *phtheiro*; this tense denotes continuous action in past time - she kept on corrupting the earth - there was no change in her future. **Immorality** is *porneia*, from which English derives "pornographic." **Blood** leaves a terrible stain, and **on her** has left out translating the Greek word *cheiros*, meaning "hand," and "on" is *ek*, which could be translated "out of," or "by." Hence, it could read, "by her hand."

Bond-servants is *doulos*, willing servants.

b. The second "Hallelujah"

> ► *And a second time they said, "Hallelujah! Her smoke rises up forever and ever" [Revelation 19:3].*

They refers back to the "great multitude" of verse 1. The Greek phrase *ochlou pollou* is identical to that in Revelation 7:9, which are probably the martyrs of Revelation 6:9-11. This great multitude may, then, be all the "saints and apostles and prophets" of all ages who have died for their faith in Christ, Revelation 18:20.

Her smoke refers back to "the great harlot" of verse 2, but notice that her smoke *rises up forever and ever*, a singular reference that supports an interpretation of Chapters 17 and 18 that they are talking about two separate cities. Forever and ever certainly describes an eternal burning, but here means that all the followers of that apostate church are burning forever and ever - *an eternal and final punishment.*

The political Babylon described in Chapter 18 is probably not mentioned here because the rest of Chapter 19 will be her final punishment. According to Revelation 19:20, the antichrist and false prophet are finally thrown into the Lake of Fire.

c. The third "Hallelujah"

> ▶ *And the twenty-four elders and the four living creatures fell down and worshiped God who sits on the throne, saying, "Amen. Hallelujah!" [Revelation 19:4].*

For a description of *the twenty-four elders*, see page 75; for *the four living creatures* see page 79. One thing is clear: these are separate from the "great multitude" of verses 1-3, which is distinguished from the "bride" in verse 7. There are obviously different groups of saved people and angels in heaven, which gives credence to the doctrine of the Rapture of the Church, a group very separated from other believers of other ages. Evidently, the Holy Scriptures reveal at least three separate groups of believers throughout Eternity Future: Israel, the Church, and The Nations.

Fell down and *worshiped* are graphic of physical posture in worship.

God who sits on the throne stresses the Sovereignty of God, and shows *Him* to be on the throne of heaven, not Satan, who has long wanted to overthrow God,

But you said in your heart, *I will ascend* to heaven; *I will raise* my throne above the stars of God, and *I will sit* on the mount of assembly in the recesses of the north. *I will ascend* above the heights of the clouds; *I will make* myself like the Most High [Isaiah. 14:13-14].

Amen is another transliterated Hebrew word, "amen" which means, "so be it," that we often use to end our prayers.

> ► *And a voice came from the throne, saying, "Give praise to our God, all you His bond-servants, you who fear Him, the small and the great" [Revelation 19:5].*

A voice came from the throne must not be the voice of God, but is probably the angel of verse 10, the first singular voice in this passage. *Give praise* is what we call a present tense durative, to express continuous, present action, as, "keep on praising God." *Bond-servants*, the same as in verse 2, are alive in heaven praising God and yet were described as martyrs in verse 2. Obviously, physical death does not stop a believer from serving God. *Fear* of God for a believer is reverential trust.

All refers to all the "bond-servants" of verse 2 and verse 5, but then describes them as *small and great*. This strongly suggests that there are what may be defined as "classes" of believers in heaven. (See comments on Revelation 19:4, page 187.) These "classes" may be formed according to their rewards, perhaps from their assignments from the Sovereign God, or possibly from the time period in which they were saved.

d. The fourth "Hallelujah"

> ► *Then I heard something like the voice of a great multitude and like the sound of many waters and like the sound of mighty peals of thunder, saying, "Hallelujah! For the Lord our God, the Almighty, reigns" [Revelation 19:6].*

I heard ... the voice is an immediate response of obedience to the command of verse 5. They did not require an explanation or further orders. If only Christians today would be that obedient to God's commands!

Like the sound of many waters is similar to Christ in Revelation 1:15, but this is the way Christianity works; people who follow Christ become more like Christ. *The Lord our God, the Almighty, reigns* is vividly demonstrated in Chapters 17 and 18 where God destroys the two Babylons with His great power.

> ▶ *Let us rejoice and be glad and give the glory to Him, for the marriage of the Lamb has come and His bride has made herself ready. It was given to her to clothe herself in fine linen, bright and clean; for the fine linen is the righteous acts of the saints. Then he said to me, "Write, 'Blessed are those who are invited to the marriage supper of the Lamb.'" And he said to me, "These are true words of God" [Revelation 19:7-9].*

The phrase, *marriage supper* comes from two Greek words: *gamos*, the same as verse 9, and *deipnon*, which is for the largest meal of the day. *Has come* and *has made* are both aorist tense verbs denoting completed action. Notice that she *has made herself ready*, a passive action. Also, *righteous acts, dikaiomata,* is plural in verse 8. Evidently, the *Bema Seat* of Christ has already occurred and the *bride* has been adorned or awarded. Furthermore, the word "bride" in Greek is *guna*, the word for woman or wife.[19] (The entire Millennium may be the wedding feast for Christ and His Bride!)

e. John is commanded to write God's invitation to the Millennium.

---

[19] The oriental wedding took place in three stages. First, the legal consummation of the union by the parents of the bride and groom, or the engagement, which was considered binding and viewed bride and groom as husband and wife. A formal divorce was required to break this betrothal. The Church is Christ's bride; she is betrothed to Him but the wedding has not yet taken place. Second, the presentation of the bride and payment of her dowry. Here the groom came to the bride's home to take her to his home for an official ceremony; this seems to correspond to the Rapture of the Church (see Matthew 25:1-13). Third, the wedding feast or supper celebration with the guests.

> ► *Then I fell at his feet to worship him. But he said to me, "Do not do that; I am a fellow servant of yours and your brethren who hold the testimony of Jesus; worship God. For the testimony of Jesus is the spirit of prophecy" [Revelation 19:10].*

Fellow servant is *sundoulos*. Angels and believers serve together.

2. Jesus Christ returns to rule the earth.

Jesus' entry into Jerusalem on a donkey's colt (see Matthew 21:1-11), is called "the Triumphal Entry." However, the real "Triumphal Entry" is found here in Revelation 19, when Jesus returns to rescue Israel and take over the earth.

a. The names of Christ prove He is qualified to rule. He is called Faithful and True.

> ► *And I saw heaven opened, and behold, a white horse, and He who sat on it is called Faithful and True, and in righteousness He judges and wages war [Revelation 19:11].*

Heaven opened is in contrast to the "closed temple" in heaven in Revelation 15:8, which immediately preceded the Bowl Judgments. Now heaven *opens* for Christ to come back and finish the judgment of God. *A white horse* is what a conquering king would ride as he invaded a country. Compare the antichrist of Revelation 6:2 who was imitating Christ.

Faithful is from *pisteuo*, often translated "believe" as in John 3:16, but can be translated "commit yourself." Christ is committed to the Word of God, Revelation 1:5. *True* is *alatheia*, which is intrinsic truth (compare John 14:6 and Revelation 3:7).

Righteousness is *dikaiosuna*, which is what is just and right with God as the standard - absolute righteousness (compare the "beast" in Revelation 13:5, 6 and 16-18). *He judges and wages war* describes Christ's Second Advent. We usually think of Christ as a gentle lamb in

His first coming. It is difficult to picture Him as "the Lion of the Tribe of Judah" (Revelation 5:5), coming as a conquering King.

He has a name we don't yet know.

> ► *His eyes are a flame of fire, and on His head are many diadems; and He has a name written on Him which no one knows except Himself [Revelation 19:12].*

Eyes ... a flame of fire is like what John saw in Revelation 1:14. Fire is a symbol of judgment in Scripture, so the eyes of Jesus Christ are the discerning eyes of judgment. He sees all and knows all. *Diadems* is *diadamata*, which are crowns worn *only* by the Son of the King (see Revelation 13:1). *A name ... which no one knows* will be revealed to His followers (Matthew 11:25-30).

His name is *The Word of God.*

> ► *He is clothed with a robe dipped in blood, and His name is called The Word of God [Revelation 19:13].*

A robe dipped in blood refers back to Christ whom John saw in Revelation 5:6 (see page 84). Here, His "robe dipped in blood" may refer to the blood of His enemies (see Isaiah. 63:1-6 and Revelation 14:20).

Word of God refers to Christ as the Incarnate Word of God.

> In the beginning was the *Word*, and the *Word* was with God, and the *Word* was God. He was in the beginning with God. All things came into being through Him, and apart from Him nothing came into being that has come into being....And the *Word* became flesh, and dwelt among us, and we saw His glory, glory as of the only begotten from the Father, full of grace and truth. John testified about Him and cried out, saying, "This was He of whom I said, 'He who comes after me has a higher rank than I, for He existed before me.' " For of His fullness we have all received, and grace upon grace.

For the Law was given through Moses; grace and truth were realized through Jesus Christ. No one has seen God at any time; the only begotten God who is in the bosom of the Father, He has explained Him [John 1:1-3, 14-18].

What was from the beginning, what we have heard, what we have seen with our eyes, what we have looked at and touched with our hands, concerning the *Word* of Life – and the life was manifested, and we have seen and testify and proclaim to you the eternal life, which was with the Father and was manifested to us – what we have seen and heard we proclaim to you also, so that you too may have fellowship with us; and indeed our fellowship is with the Father, and with His Son Jesus Christ. These things we write, so that our joy may be made complete [1 John 1:1-4].

The *Word* is both Creator and Judge of the earth.

> ► *And the armies which are in heaven, clothed in fine linen, white and clean, were following Him on white horses [Revelation 19:14].*

The armies, plural, are the armies of saints (Revelation 6:9; 18:20; 19:1), and angels (Revelation 7:11), which follow Him on white horses.

Clothed in white linen obviously includes the Bride of Christ, verse 7, and is obviously *not* the Rapture. From verse 10 we learned that angels and believers are "fellow servants" of the Lord Jesus Christ and together make up these armies.

> ► *From His mouth comes a sharp sword, so that with it He may strike down the nations, and He will rule them with a rod of iron; and He treads the wine press of the fierce wrath of God, the Almighty [Revelation 19:15].*

His mouth has created the world (see the eight "God saids" in Genesis 1:1-26, Psalm 33:6-9, and Hebrews 11:3). **Sword** is *rhomphaia*, which was a very long, two-handed sword used in battle (see Revelation 1:16).

For *the nations* see Matthew 25:31-46, Isaiah. 64:1, 2, and Psalm 2:1-12. *Strike down the nations* is *not* the Rapture (see Zechariah 14:1-11).

A rod of iron is unyielding and firm. *He treads the wine press of the fierce wrath of God the Almighty* shows that God's grace for these Christ-rejectors is past (see Revelation 14:19; 15:7 and 16:19).

His name is King of kings and Lord of lords.

> ► *And on His robe and on His thigh He has a name written, "King of kings, and Lord of lords"[Revelation 19:16].*

King of kings and Lord of lords is that well-known title for Christ, which shows that He was born to rule.

> Where is He who has been born *King* of the Jews? For we saw His star in the east and have come to worship Him [Matthew 2:2].

b. The deeds of Christ prove He is qualified to rule.

> ► *Then I saw an angel standing in the sun, and he cried out with a loud voice, saying to all the birds which fly in midheaven, "Come, assemble for the great supper of God" [Revelation 19:17].*

He commands the *birds* of the earth. *An angel* is another powerful angel as in verse 10 and may be the angel of Revelation 16:8 who poured his bowl into the sun. *Standing in the sun* probably means that his shining is now brighter than the sun. *Midheaven* is the atmosphere where the birds normally fly (see Revelation 14:6).

Come is imperative mood, the mood of command, and whenever God commands His "lower creation" they always obey; it is His higher creation of man and angels who disobey God. *Supper* is *deipnon,* the same as in Revelation 14:9, but here it is the *mega*, or *great* supper of God.

> ▶ *(S)o that you may eat the flesh of kings and the flesh of commanders and the flesh of mighty men and the flesh of horses and of those who sit on them and the flesh of all men, both free men and slaves, and small and great [Revelation 19:18].*

Verse 18 describes the ranks within the armies of man assembled at Armageddon against God: **kings, commanders, mighty men,** and the cavalry, **those who sit on them.** Then John describes the classes of people who are gathered to watch the destruction of Israel; **all men, both free men and slaves, and small and great.** The so-called innocent bystanders who are also Christ-rejectors will be caught up in the slaughter.

c. Christ easily defeats the antichrist and false prophet.

> ▶ *And I saw the beast and the kings of the earth and their armies assembled to make war against Him who sat on the horse and against His army [Revelation 19:19].*

The beast is the antichrist of Revelation 13:1-10 and 2 Thessalonians 2:8 who is now the self-appointed general of all the world's armies. They **assembled to make war against Him** (Christ) **who sat on the horse.** They came to Israel to annihilate that nation, but as they see Christ coming from heaven, they turn to try and defeat Him. It is the ultimate in pride, to think that they can defeat God. **His army** of saints never fights; Christ and His holy angels do all the fighting. Probably, the "sharp sword" from His mouth relates to the commands He issues to His holy angels who attack the human armies. Possibly these angels use swords to chop off the heads of the soldiers, which explains why all their blood runs "as deep as the horses' bridles" (Revelation 14:20). They have been chopping off the heads of the saints (Revelation 20:4), and now they suffer the same fate.

> Do not be deceived, God is not mocked, for whatever a man sows, that shall he also reap [Galatians 6:7].

> ► *And the beast was seized, and with him the false*
> *prophet who performed the signs in his presence, by*
> *which he deceived those who had received the mark of*
> *the beast and those who worshipped his image; these*
> *two were thrown alive into the lake of fire which burns*
> *with brimstone [Revelation 19:20].*

The beast was seized ... and *thrown alive into the lake of fire*. This shows that the supreme ruler of the satanic world system is not exempt from the judgment of God. A person's standing in the world will not spare him or her from the judgment of God.

The false prophet is the same as Revelation 13:11-16 and is called "false" because he led people to the antichrist, the false christ, which is idolatry. Any worship short of Jesus Christ, the true God, is idolatry. These two were *thrown alive into the lake of fire* at the onset of the Millennium (see Revelation 19:20) and, according to Revelation 20:10, after 1000 years they are still in residence. What a terrifying final judgment this is for them!

Christ easily kills all the armies of the beast.

> ► *And the rest were killed with the sword which came*
> *from the mouth of Him who sat on the horse, and all*
> *the birds were filled with their flesh [Revelation*
> *19:21].*

The rest is all the followers of the beast and false prophet who were quickly dealt with in verses 19-20. To defeat an army completely, its commander must be conquered. This usually occurs last, but Jesus in this case does it first. *All the birds were filled with their flesh* shows the total conquest of the conquering king.

> For just as the lightning comes from the east and
> flashes even to the west, so will the coming of the Son
> of Man be. Wherever the corpse is, there the vultures
> will gather. But immediately after the tribulation of
> those days the sun will be darkened, and the moon will
> not give its light, and the stars will fall from the sky,
> and the powers of the heavens will be shaken. And

then the sign of the Son of Man will appear in the sky, and then all the tribes of the earth will mourn, and they will see the Son of Man coming on the clouds of the sky with power and great glory. And He will send forth His angels with a great trumpet and they will gather together His elect from the four winds, from one end of the sky to the other [Matthew 24:27-31 (see also Revelation 16:12-16)].

Jesus puts down the unrighteous because He will rule and reign in total righteousness.

D. The Millennium and the Great White Throne Judgment, Revelation 20:1-15.

Following His Second Advent, Christ establishes some rather drastic changes with His rule over the earth. Some of these occurred in Chapter 19 and more will appear in Chapter 20. Chapter 19 is both climactic and transitional. The entire Book of the Revelation (especially Chapters 6-18) prepares us for Chapter 19, which fits with the theme of the book, therefore, it is climactic. Chapter 19 is also transitional to the supreme rule of Christ for the first 1,000 years over the earth. Part of this rule is described in verses 1-6, where John gives details on the very beginning of Christ's millennial reign. In verses 7-15, John gives details on the very ending of this reign. For more detail of what conditions are like in between, refer to Psalm 72, Isaiah 2, Isaiah 11, and Zechariah 14.

1. At the first of the Millennium, Christ binds Satan and resurrects believers, Revelation 20:1-6.

a. The Devil is bound to stop his deception.

> ► *Then I saw an angel coming down from heaven, holding the key of the abyss and a great chain in his hand [Revelation 20:1].*

And I saw is the fourth time this phrase occurs (see Revelation 19:11, 17 and 19). Thus, John is continuing the sequence of events that he saw started in Revelation 19:11, the Second Advent of Christ. *An angel* is another heavenly angel as is the one in Revelation 19:17. Some speculate this to be Michael, the archangel (see Jude 9), the only angel more powerful than Satan.

The key of the abyss had already been given to Satan to loose demons (see Revelation 9:1-3), but now a *holy angel* has the key and Satan will be put into the same prison-house for demons that he himself opened earlier. *Abyss* is *abussos*, which means "shaft," "bottomless" or "bottomless pit." It is probably a compartment of Hades (see footnote 16, page 108).

> And Jesus asked him, "What is your name?" And he said, "Legion"; for many demons had entered him. They were imploring Him not to command them to go away into the *abyss* [Luke 8:30, 31].

> ... Do not say in your heart, "Who will ascend into heaven?" (that is, to bring Christ down), or, "Who will descend into the *abyss*?"... [Romans 10:6b, 7a].

> For if God did not spare angels when they sinned, but cast them into *hell* and committed them to pits of darkness, reserved for judgment [2 Peter 2:4].

The Greek word for "hell" is *tartaros*, found only here in the Greek New Testament. "Deep abyss" would be a better translation.

The *great chain* must be a very special chain that will hold a spiritual being like Satan.

> ► *And he laid hold of the dragon, the serpent of old, who is the devil and Satan, and bound him for a thousand years [Revelation 20:2].*

Dragon is from the root *derkomai*, which means "to see." A dragon was a fierce creature that could see in all directions and was impossible to sneak up on. *The serpent of old* refers back to Genesis 3:1-24 when Satan came into the Garden of Eden in the form of a serpent. *Devil* is *diabolos*, which means "accuser" (see Revelation 12:10). *Satan* is *satan*, "adversary."

Be of sober spirit, be on the alert. Your *adversary*, the devil, prowls around like a roaring lion, seeking someone to devour [1 Peter 5:8].

Bound is an aorist indicative active from the Greek, *deo*, which means to bind, tie, confine, impede, hinder. The interpretation of this word by amillennialists and post-millennialists is that during the Church Age Satan is "bound" or at least "hindered." These doctrinal positions interpret the Millennium to be occurring *during* the Church Age. They do not take the "thousand years" literally, but allegorize it to simply mean a long period of time. However, in all of Scripture whenever a day or month or year is used with a numeral it is always meant *literally*; such as, the "seventy-years-captivity" of Israel (see Jeremiah 25:11, 12), or "the-third-day" resurrection of Christ (see Matthew 16:21).

► *(A)nd threw him into the abyss, and shut it and sealed it over him, so that he would not deceive the nations any longer, until the thousand years were completed; after these things he must be released for a short time [Revelation 20:3].*

Threw him into the abyss, and shut it and sealed it over him, so that he would not deceive the nations any longer does not sound like Satan is merely "hindered," but rather is truly *bound* and *unable* to deceive the nations or individuals. *The thousand years* appears here the second of six times in six verses. *Deceive* is *planao*, which means to seduce, to wander, to lead astray, Revelation 12:9. *Released for a short time* predicts the following verses (Revelation 20:7-10), when Satan will be allowed to deceive the nations once more, but only for a limited time.

b. Believers are resurrected to begin their reign with Christ.

► *Then I saw thrones, and they sat on them, and judgment was given to them. And I saw the souls of those who had been beheaded because of their testimony of Jesus and because of the word of God, and those who had not worshipped the beast or his image, and had not received the mark on their forehead and on their hand; and they came to life and reigned with Christ for a thousand years [Revelation 20:4].*

Then I saw continues the sequence of events. **They** is understood from the plural verb "sat upon," and refers back to Revelation 19:14, "the armies which are in heaven." These "armies" include the Old Testament saints, the "bride" (Revelation 19:7); then a third group of tribulation saints will join them as described in the rest of this verse, *the souls of those who had been beheaded* (see Revelation 6:9-11). This third group has *suffered*: *beheaded ... not worshiped the beast ... not received the mark.* Now they will *rule: they came to life and reigned with Christ for a thousand years.*

Came to life and **reigned** are both aorist tense verbs denoting completed action. Amillennialist doctrine argues that "came to life" refers to the regeneration experience of a believer during the Church Age and that it does not refer to bodily resurrection. However, in Revelation 1:18 and 2:8 the same word is used to refer to the resurrected Jesus Christ; *He certainly experienced bodily resurrection!*

The tribulation saints are a model of true Christian living: we must suffer now, but later will rule and reign with Christ.

► *The rest of the dead did not come to life until the thousand years were completed. This is the first resurrection [Revelation 20:5].*

The sentence, *the rest of the dead did not come to life until the thousand years were completed* is better understood as translated in the NIV as a parenthesis. It is completely separate from the *first resurrection*, which includes the tribulation saints in verse 4. "The first resurrection" has actually been completed in three stages:

(1) The resurrection of Christ as the firstfruits ...

But now Christ has been raised from the dead, the *first fruits* of those who are asleep [1 Corinthians 15:20].

... and a few Old Testament saints;

The tombs were opened, and many *bodies of the saints who had fallen asleep* were raised; and coming out of the tombs after His resurrection they entered the holy city and appeared to many [Matthew 27:52, 53].

(2) The future Rapture of the Church

But we do not want you to be uninformed, brethren, about *those who are asleep*, so that you will not grieve as do the rest who have no hope. For if we believe that Jesus died and rose again, even so God will bring with Him those who have fallen asleep in Jesus. For this we say to you by the word of the Lord, that we who are alive and remain until the coming of the Lord, will not precede *those who have fallen asleep*. For the Lord Himself will descend from heaven with a shout, with the voice of the archangel and with the trumpet of God, and the *dead in Christ* will rise first. Then we who are alive and remain will be caught up together with them in the clouds to meet the Lord in the air, and so we shall always be with the Lord [1 Thessalonians 4:13-17].

(3) The resurrection of the tribulation Saints and the rest of the Old Testament Saints at the Second Advent of Christ

Now at that time Michael, the great prince who stands guard over the sons of your people, will arise. And there will be a time of distress such as never occurred since there was a nation until that time; and at that time your people, everyone who is found written in the book, will be rescued. Many of *those who sleep in the dust of the ground* will awake, these to everlasting life, but the others to disgrace and everlasting contempt [Daniel 12:1, 2].

For as in Adam all die, so also in Christ all will be made alive. But each in his own order: Christ the first fruits, after that *those who are Christ's at His first coming*, then comes the end, when He hands over the kingdom to the God and Father, when He has abolished all rule and authority and power [I Corinthians 15:22-24].

Then I saw thrones, and they sat on them, and judgment was given to them. And I saw the *souls of those who had been beheaded* because of their testimony of Jesus and because of the word of God, and those who had not worshipped the beast or his image, and had not received the mark on their forehead and on their hand; and they came to life and reigned with Christ for a thousand years [Revelation 20:4].

Amillennial doctrine holds that this "first resurrection" is when a person is born-again by trusting in Jesus Christ as personal Savior during the Church Age. Thus, it is maintained that this "first resurrection" will spare them from the second death brought up in verse 6. Such erroneous interpretations result from not taking the *thousand years* literally.

▶ *Blessed and holy is the one who has a part in the first resurrection; over these the second death has no power, but they will be priests of God and Christ and will reign with Him for a thousand years [Revelation 20:6].*[20]

Blessed is *makarios*, which means to be supernaturally blessed. *Holy* is *hagios*, meaning to be set apart (by the blood of Christ, not by good works). *The second death* is identified as "the Lake of Fire" in verse 14 and in Revelation 21:8.

Priests are those who intercede for others before God. *Will reign* ties back to verse 4, which says, "judgment was given to them." For the twelve apostles it will mean judging the twelve tribes of Israel.

(A)nd just as My Father has granted Me a kingdom, I grant you that you may eat and drink at My table in My kingdom, and you will sit on thrones judging the

---

[20] See illustration seven, the two resurrections.

Illustration Seven – Two Resurrections in Scripture

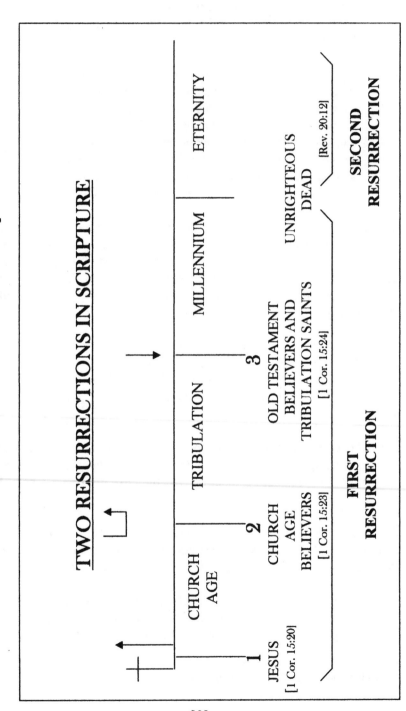

Twelve tribes of Israel [Luke 2:29, 30].

Or do you not know that the *saints will judge the world?* If the world is judged by you, are you not competent to constitute the smallest law courts? Do you not know that *we will judge angels?* How much more matters in this life? [1 Corinthians 6:2,3].

The fallen angels who have followed Satan in his rebellion are not mentioned in the Book of the Revelation again. Perhaps these fallen angels are judged by the saints during the Millennium and cast into the Lake of Fire, because that is exactly where they end up.

Then He will also say to those on His left, "Depart from Me, accursed ones, into the *eternal fire* which has been prepared for the devil and his angels" [Matthew 25:41].

2. At the last of the Millennium, Christ judges Satan and all unbelievers, Revelation 20:7-15.

a. The devil is loosed to renew his deception.

▶ *When the thousand years are completed, Satan will be released from his prison [Revelation 20:7].*

For *the thousand years,* see page 198. Taken literally, this "thousand years" is the seventh dispensation or time period in the overall plan of God. This dispensation is called the Millennium (Latin, *mille* for 1,000 plus *annum* for years: therefore, a millennium is 1,000 years), also called the *Golden Age,* or the *Kingdom Age.*

Amillennial and postmillennial doctrines insist that Satan is *now* bound during the Church Age. Scripture suggests otherwise:

But Peter said, "Ananias, why has *Satan filled your heart* to lie to the Holy Spirit and to keep back some of the price of the land?" [Acts 5:3].

(A)nd said, "You who are *full of all deceit and fraud*, you son of the devil, you enemy of all righteousness, will you not cease to make crooked the straight ways of the Lord?" [Acts 13:10].

I have decided to *deliver such a one to Satan* for the destruction of his flesh, so that his spirit may be saved in the day of the Lord Jesus [1 Corinthians 5:5].

Because of the surpassing greatness of the revelations, for this reason, to keep me from exalting myself, there was given me a thorn in the flesh, *a messenger of Satan* to torment me – to keep me from exalting myself! [2 Corinthians 12:7].

Submit therefore to God. *Resist the devil* and he will flee from you [James 4:7].

Do not fear what you are about to suffer. Behold, the *devil is about to cast some of you into prison*, so that you will be tested, and you will have tribulation for ten days. Be faithful unto death, and I will give you the crown of life [Revelation 2:10].

If Satan is bound now, he must have a very long chain indeed!

Are completed is an aorist subjunctive passive from *teleo*, which means to finish, to complete, to conclude. The subjunctive mood is the mood of contingency or condition; the condition is the full thousand years, because Satan will not be released until those years are complete. But why release him at all? Why not just keep him bound up forever and ever? Simply put, man has always been subject to the wiles of the devil, ever since the Garden of Eden. It has been Satan who offered man the alternative to knowing and serving God. Christ rules the world with a rod of iron throughout the Millennium demonstrating His power and right to rule the nations.

Ask of Me, and I will surely give the nations as *Your inheritance*, and the very ends of the earth as *Your*

possession. You shall break them with a rod of iron,
You shall shatter them like earthenware [Psalm 2:8-9].

Mankind will have to obey Christ outwardly, but not necessarily inwardly; so, Satan will be released this one last time to provide all men and women born during the Millennium a choice; obey Christ or follow Satan. God never judges man strictly upon heart attitude, but also by his works. Works reveal the condition of the heart, so the Christ-rejectors from the Millennium will be given their chance to show the true condition of their heart.

> ▶ *(A)nd will come out to deceive the nations which are in the four corners of the earth, Gog and Magog, to gather them together for the war; the number of them is like the sand of the seashore [Revelation 20:8].*

Deceive is *planao* (see also page 139, Revelation 12:9), which means to seduce, to wander, to lead astray.

The nations which are in the four corners of the earth is John's way of saying this is yet another *worldwide* rebellion. Such world-wide rebellion is what brings the wrath of God, evident from the events of the Tribulation. **Gog and Magog** are two titles that Ezekiel used to describe the leaders and the followers of Russia when they invade Israel in Ezekiel 38-39. John uses those same titles here to describe the leader and followers of this newest rebellion against God and their invasion of Israel.

The number of them is like the sand of the seashore describes an innumerable army that aligns itself with Satan. Notice there is no mention of demons: perhaps they have all been judged by the Christians (1 Corinthians 6:3), and are now in the Lake of Fire. Evidently, most of the people born in the Millennium are not "born-again" and follow in the rebellion against Christ.

> Enter through the narrow gate; for the gate is wide and the way is broad that leads to destruction, and there are many who enter through it. For the gate is small and the way is narrow that leads to life, and there are few who find it [Matthew 7:13, 14].

This principle that Jesus taught will also be true during the Millennium.

> ► *And they came up on the broad plain of the earth and surrounded the camp of the saints and the beloved city, and fire came down from heaven and devoured them [Revelation 20:9].*

The broad plain of the earth is unidentifiable, unless John is talking about the valley of Jezreel, Revelation 16:16, or Armageddon, which the devil might use again. However, the typography of the land has been drastically changed (see Revelation 16:20), so that Jerusalem is now surrounded by a "broad plain."

Surrounded is a Greek military term, *kukleuo*, which means to encamp against, to encircle (in battle array). Again the devil seeks to destroy the people of God here described as **the saints**, which is *hagioi*, meaning "set apart ones." "Saints" are set apart by their faith in the blood of Christ, not by their good deeds. They have good deeds later because they are saints.

The beloved city is Jerusalem, the world headquarters of Christ. **Fire came down from heaven and devoured them** just as at Sodom and Gomorrah in Genesis 18. Again, the Lord does the fighting for His people as in Revelation 19:15.

b. The Devil is judged into the Lake of Fire.

> ► *And the devil who deceived them was thrown into the lake of fire and brimstone, where the beast and false prophet are also; and they will be tormented day and night forever and ever [Revelation 20:10].*

Devil is *diabolos*, "accuser" (see Revelation 12:10). **Who deceived them** shows that while they may be fooled, man is still held responsible by God for their behavior. The word **brimstone** is here added to the description of the Lake of Fire; it is *theion*, which means sulphur. Sulphur burns in air with a blue flame and suffocating odor. It is used in making gunpowder and matches, as well as certain ointments and medicines. The judgment of the devil already took place at the Cross where the perfect tense is used; "has been judged," past action with present, on-going results.

> (A)nd concerning judgment, because *the ruler of this world has been judged* [John 16:11].

Where the beast and the false prophet are also shows that the antichrist and the false prophet, who were thrown into the Lake of Fire at the beginning of the Millennium (Revelation 19:20), are still *alive* in it. The Bible does not teach that Christ-rejectors are annihilated; they are forever tortured in the Lake of Fire. *They will be tormented* includes the devil and humans who have rebelled against God. *Forever and ever* is the phrase *eis tous aionas ton aionon*, which literally translates as *to the ages of the ages*; it was the strongest way a Greek could describe eternity.

c. The Christ-rejectors are judged into the Lake of Fire.

> ► *Then I saw a great white throne and Him who sat upon it, from whose presence earth and heaven fled away, and no place was found for them [Revelation 20:11].*

Then I saw continues the context. *Throne* is used 30 times in the Book of the Revelation, but this is the first time it is called a *white* throne. It shows the purity and holiness of God as the Supreme Judge. *Him who sat upon it* is Jesus Christ because God the Father has entrusted all judgment to His Son; the phrase denotes the greatest of power and authority.

> For not even the Father judges anyone, but He has *given all judgment to the Son* [John 5:22].

Just as the *bema seat* is a separate throne, so the Great White Throne may also be a separate one that God will use for this particular judgment.

For *from whose presence earth and heaven fled away;*

But the day of the Lord will come like a thief, in which the *heavens will pass away* with a roar and the elements will be destroyed with intense heat, and the earth and its works will be burned up. Since all these things are to be destroyed in this way, what sort of people ought you to be in holy conduct and godliness [2 Peter 3:10,11].

Christ will judge all Christ-rejectors before He creates the New Heaven and the New Earth. *No place was found for them* because Christ-rejectors are always trying to get away from the Lamb (Revelation 6:15, 16).

> ► *And I saw the dead, the great and the small, standing before the throne, and books were opened; and another book was opened, which is the book of life; and the dead were judged from the things which were written in the books, according to their deeds [Revelation 20:12].*

The dead are the unrighteous dead, the unbelievers of every age, not just those of the Millennium. **The great and small** shows that every level of society is there, none will escape. The only way to have escaped this judgment was to have trusted in Christ.

> Truly, truly, I say to you, he who hears My word, and believes Him who sent Me, has eternal life, and does *not come into judgment*, but has passed out of death into life. Truly, truly, I say to you, an hour is coming and now is, when the dead will hear the voice of the Son of God, and those who hear will live. For just as the Father has life in Himself, even so He gave to the Son also to have life in Himself; and He gave Him authority to execute judgment, because He is the Son of Man. Do not marvel at this, for an hour is coming, in which all who are in the tombs will hear His voice, and will come forth; those who did the good deeds to a resurrection of life, those who committed the evil deeds to a resurrection of judgment [John 5:24-29].

Do not work for the food which perishes, but for the food which endures to eternal life, which the Son of Man will give to you, for on Him the Father, God, has set His seal. Therefore they said to Him, "What shall we do, so that we may work the works of God?" Jesus answered and said to them, "This is the work of God, that you *believe in Him whom He has sent*" [John 6:27-29].

Standing before the throne shows these unrighteous dead have been resurrected, not with a resurrection body as believers have, but with one that will *endure forever* the physical punishment of the Lake of Fire. ***Books*** are books of recorded deeds, ***according to their deeds*** or works (see Luke 20:46, 47). Their deeds will determine how far down they go into the Lake of Fire, because God is a God of perfect justice.

Beware of the scribes, who like to walk around in long robes, and *love respectful greetings* in the market place, and chief seats in the synagogues and places of honor at banquets, who *devour widows' houses*, and for appearance's sake *offer long prayers. These will receive greater condemnation* [Luke 20:46, 47].

The ***Book of Life*** has the names of each person who trusted in Christ as personal Savior.

Nevertheless do not rejoice in this, that the spirits are subject to you, but rejoice that your *names are recorded in heaven* [Luke 10:20].

Indeed, true companion, I ask you also to help these women who have shared my struggle in the cause of the gospel, together with Clement also and the rest of my fellow workers, whose names are in *the book of life* [Philippians 4:3].

He who overcomes will thus be clothed in white garments; and I will not erase his name from *the book of life* ... [Revelation 3:5a].

All who dwell on the earth will worship him (antichrist), everyone whose name has not been written from the foundation of the world in *the book of life* of the Lamb who has been slain [Revelation 13:8].

(A)nd nothing unclean, and no one who practices abomination and lying, shall ever come into it, but only those whose names are written in the Lamb's *book of life* [Revelation 21:27].

Judged is *krino*, which basically means to separate. It is also what "death" means (see verse 14; the "Second Death," being separated from the grace of God for all eternity). There are 42 references in the New Testament regarding a judgment contingent upon works.

▶ *And the sea gave up the dead which were in it, and death and Hades gave up the dead which were in them; and they were judged, every one of them according to their deeds [Revelation 20:13].*

Death is the first death - spiritual death - that the unbeliever has experienced. *Hades* is the place of the dead. *Every one* is the Greek *hekastos*, which means each one. *No one escapes.*

▶ *Then death and Hades were thrown into the lake of fire. This is the second death, the lake of fire [Revelation 20:14].*

The second death is a *place*, "the Lake of Fire."

▶ *And if anyone's name was not found written in the book of life, he was thrown into the lake of fire [Revelation 20:15].*

Was thrown is aorist tense, completed action.

For we know Him who said, "Vengeance is mine, I will repay." And again, "The Lord *will judge* His people." It is a terrifying thing to fall into the hands of the living God [Hebrews 10:30, 31].

E. The New Heaven, the New Earth, and the New Jerusalem, Revelation 21:1-27.

Here John continues the sequence with the seventh occurrence of "and I saw." He began using this phrase back in Revelation 19:11 to describe the Second Advent of Christ. Christ has made some drastic changes beginning with His Second Advent.

Now, with the completion of the Great White Throne Judgment (Revelation 20:11-15), Jesus will create a New Heaven and a New Earth. The New Jerusalem was probably there during the Millennium as a satellite city, hovering over the "old" Jerusalem that was on the earth.

1. God creates a New Heaven and a New Earth.

> ► *Then I saw a new heaven and a new earth; for the first heaven and the first earth passed away, and there is no longer any sea [Revelation 21:1].*

Then I saw is the seventh time John uses this phrase since Revelation 19:11. ***New*** is *kainos,* which denotes that which is unaccustomed or unused, not new in time, not recent, but new as to form or quality, of different nature from what is contrasted as old (see Romans 8:18-23).

First indicates there must be a second. ***Passed away*** is the Greek *aperchomai,* a different verb from *pheugo* in Revelation 20:11, which is translated "fled away." ***Passed away*** is an aorist indicative active (completed action), which could be translated "disappeared" (see 2 Peter 3:5-13).

No longer any sea is in contrast to the only river (Revelation 22:1), which is the River of Life. Also, "sea" in the Book of the Revelation is used both literally and figuratively. In Revelation 13:1 it is the source of the "beast," referring to the Gentiles. Then, in Revelation 20:3, it was a place of the dead. Such connotations will *not* be allowed in the New Earth. Assumedly, the cycle of evaporation and rainfall will not be necessary as it was in the Millennium.

And it will be that whichever of the families of the earth does not go up to Jerusalem to worship the King, the LORD of hosts, there will be *no rain* on them [Zechariah 14:17].

2. In the New Jerusalem, God will dwell with His people.

> ▶ *And I saw the holy city, new Jerusalem, coming down out of heaven from God, made ready as a bride adorned for her husband [Revelation 21:2].*

And I saw is repeated. *Holy* was also used to describe the earthly Jerusalem of the Millennium. It is *hagios*, which means to be set apart. *New* is *kainos* as in verse 1 (see page 211).

Coming down is a present participle, "descending." The New Jerusalem probably hovers over the old Jerusalem during the Millennium. Waiting for the Rapture, Jesus is preparing places for believers to live in the New Jerusalem.

> Do not let your heart be troubled; believe in God, believe also in Me. In My Father's house are *many dwelling places*; if it were not so, I would have told you; for I go to prepare a place for you. If I go and prepare a place for you, I will come again and receive you to myself, that where I am, there you may be also [John 14:1-3].

However, during the Millennium, before the old earth passed away, there was not a place for the New Jerusalem on earth. Those who participated in the first resurrection (Revelation 20:6) will live in the satellite city, moving back and forth from the New Jerusalem to earth, serving Christ who will be ruling from David's throne in the old Jerusalem.

Out of heaven from God supports the idea that the saints have been in "My Father's house."

Made ready and *adorned* are both perfect passive participles that denote past action with present, on-going results. Passive means *her* has received the action of the verb. Notice that it does *not* say that the New Jerusalem is *the* bride, but adorned *as* a bride.

Adorned is the verb *kosmeo*, from which we derive the English word "cosmetic." It means to make beautiful, to make attractive. Perhaps a clearer translation would be, "having been made ready as a bride who has been made beautiful." These participles give the idea that the New Jerusalem has been around long before this point.

> ▶ *And I heard a loud voice from the throne, saying, "Behold, the tabernacle of God is among men, and He will dwell among them, and they shall be His people, and God Himself will be among them" [Revelation 21:3].*

A loud voice occurs here for the last of 21 times. It has been something John heard which was emphasizing something important. **The throne** is the one John saw back in Revelation 20:11 (see page 207), which is the *Great White Throne*. Judgment is finished from that throne, and now an announcement of great grace is made, **God is among men**. This is exactly what God has wanted ever since the Garden of Eden.

> They heard the sound of the LORD God *walking in the garden* in the cool of the day, and the man and his wife hid themselves from the presence of the LORD God among the trees of the garden. Then the LORD God called to the man, and said to him, "Where are you?" He said, "I heard the sound of You in the garden, and I was afraid because I was naked; so I hid myself [Genesis 3:8-10].

The LORD God was the pre-incarnate Christ who came every day to commune with Adam and Eve, because He has always wanted to be among us. But Adam and Eve hid from the LORD God because they had sinned.

Tabernacle is from the verb *skanoo*, which includes the idea of fellowship, to have a blessing. **Dwell** is the same verb *skanoo*; here is what we call a future durative; it carries the idea of "shall keep on dwelling." There will be no sinful interruption as in the Garden of Eden.

People is *laos*, which is literally "peoples." We translate it as a collective noun, but in the plural it actually includes *all* the different peoples of the redeemed of the earth. The verb *skanoo* also means, "to live in a tent."

> ► *(A)nd He will wipe away every tear from their eyes; and there will no longer be any death; there will no longer be any mourning, or crying, or pain; the first things have passed away [Revelation 21:4].*

And He will wipe away every tear occurs *after* all the judgments. This strongly suggests that there will be tears in heaven for a while, but God promises that He will wipe them all away. **Wipe away** can be translated "wipe out" and means to abolish. Some interpret this phrase to be a general statement of God's comfort, and does not suggest any failure of the saints in *bema seat* judgment. However, if we compare Revelation 7:17 and 6:9-11, we do find tearful situations described in heaven.

Every tear is *pas dakruon*, literally "all tear" with the single noun "tear," so we translate "every" for "all." Four of the major causes of tears are here described as being ***no longer***: ***death, mourning, crying, pain***. It is difficult to imagine life without these four things that we have always had to deal with. *Crying* is *krazo*, meaning to cry out, to weep aloud, and is the same word found in heaven back in Revelation 6:10 (see also John 11:35, where the Greek word is *dakruo*, which means to weep, shed tears).

> ► *And He who sits on the throne said, "Behold, I am making all things new." And He said, "Write, for these words are faithful and true" [Revelation 21:5].*

He who sits on the throne is the Lord Jesus Christ (Revelation 20:11). ***Behold*** is *idou* (the same as in verse 3) in the imperative from *orao*, which means to look, to see. Imperative is the mood of command. ***I am making*** means "to make, form, construct."

> Therefore if anyone is in Christ, he is a new creature, the old things passed away; behold, *new things have come* [2 Corinthians 5:17].

> For *by Him all things were created*, both in the heavens and on earth, visible and invisible, whether thrones or dominions or rulers or authorities – all things have been created through Him and for Him [Colossians 1:16].

All things are in the new heaven and new earth, and God will give these "things" to His children, verse 7 (See also Romans 8:18-25).

John is now *commanded* to "write" (as in Revelation 19:9) because back in Revelation 10:4 there were some things John was commanded *not to write*.

These words are faithful and true because they are the words of Christ.

> Jesus said to him, "I am the way, and the *truth*, and the life; no one comes to the Father but through Me" [John 14:6].

> ▶ *Then He said to me, "It is done. I am the Alpha and Omega, the beginning and the end. I will give to the one who thirsts from the spring of the water of life without cost" [Revelation 21:6].*

It is done is not *tetelistai*, which Jesus said from the Cross. This is *gegonan*, the perfect form of *ginomai*, which means to bring into existence by creation. Jesus is now finished creating the New Heaven, the New Earth, and the New Jerusalem. Unlike the old, these will never wear out.

I am is a Biblical description of Deity. *Alpha and Omega* are the first and last letters of the Greek alphabet. In Revelation 1:8, Jesus used this to describe Himself and refers to *His* eternality. Conversely, Satan is *not* eternal, he was created (see Ezekiel 28:13).

You had the seal of perfection, full of wisdom and perfect in beauty. You were in Eden, the garden of God; every precious stone was your covering...on the day that *you were created* they were prepared [Ezekiel 28:12b, 13a, c].

The beginning and the end also describes Christ's Sovereignty and His right to rule over every part of His creation.

I will give can be compared to John 6:27-29 to see that salvation is a gift from God, it cannot be earned (see also Ephesians 2:8, 9).

... they said to Him, "What shall we do, so that we may work the works of God?" Jesus answered and said to them, "This is the work of God, that you believe in Him whom He has sent" [John 6:28b, 29].

For by grace you have been saved through faith; and that not of yourselves, it is the *gift* of God; not as a result of works, so that no one may boast [Ephesians 2:8,9].

Notice the *without cost* at the end of verse 6 (see John 4:13, 14; in Jesus' conversation with the woman at the well He promises to give eternal life).

Jesus answered and said to her, "Everyone who drinks of this water will thirst again; but whoever drinks of the water that I will give him shall never thirst; but the water that I will give him will become in him a well of water springing up to eternal life" [John 4:13, 14].

▶ *He who overcomes will inherit these things, and I will be his God and he will be My son [Revelation 21:7].*

He who overcomes is a believer in Christ.

For whatever is born of God *overcomes* the world; and this is the victory that has *overcome* the world – our faith. Who is the one who *overcomes* the world, but he who believes that Jesus is the Son of God? [1 John 5:4,5].

Now to Him who is able to keep you from stumbling, and to make you stand in the presence of His glory blameless with great joy, to the only God our Savior, through Jesus Christ our Lord, be glory, majesty, dominion and authority, before all time and now and forever, Amen. [Jude 24, 25].

Will inherit these things was predicted by Paul in 1 Corinthians 3:21-23 and by John in Revelation 6:9-11. Christ Himself is part of our inheritance.

So then let no one boast in men. For *all things belong to you*, whether Paul or Apollo or Cephas or the world or life or death or things present or things to come; *all things belong to you*, and you belong to Christ; and Christ belongs to God [1 Corinthians 3:21-23 (See also Revelation 6:9-11)].

My son is taught in John 1:12 as referring to believers in Christ.

But as many as received Him, to them he gave the right to become *children of God*, even to those who believe in His name [John 1:12].

▶ *But for the cowardly and unbelieving and abominable and murderers and immoral persons and sorcerers and idolaters and all liars, their part will be in the lake that burns with fire and brimstone, which is the second death [Revelation 21:8].*

This list of horrible behavior is evidence that no conversion took place for the people here described. Paul gives a similar description of believers *before* they were saved.

Or do you not know that the unrighteous will not inherit the kingdom of God? Do not be deceived, neither fornicators, nor idolaters, nor adulterers, nor effeminate, nor homosexuals, nor thieves, nor the covetous, nor drunkards, nor revilers, nor swindlers will inherit the kingdom of God [1 Corinthians 6:9-11].

Abominable is *bdelusso*, meaning to be detestable, to pollute, to defile. *Immoral* is *pornos*, which gives our word "pornography." *Sorcerers* is from *pharmakos*, drugs used in magic.

3. The New Jerusalem will be glorious.

Since all the believers of every age will have access to the New Jerusalem, verse 24, and since those who live there are called "sons of God," verse 7, God has carefully made this city truly magnificent! God has made a city that from every aspect will reflect His glory.

a. The New Jerusalem reflects the glory of God.

> ► *Then one of the seven angels who had the seven bowls full of the seven last plagues came and spoke with me, saying, "Come here, I will show you the bride, the wife of the Lamb" [Revelation 21:9].*

Last plagues shows that God's wrath will be poured out in a final judgment; the earth will not have to face God's wrath again because Christ will be on the throne. Compare *the bride, the wife of the Lamb* in this verse with "the holy city, Jerusalem" in the next verse; God does not separate His bride from where she dwells. A woman gets part of her self-image from the house she lives in; therefore, Christ furnishes His bride with a magnificent dwelling place.

> ► *And he carried me away in the Spirit to a great and high mountain, and showed me the holy city, Jerusalem, coming down out of heaven from God [Revelation 21:10].*

In the Spirit is capitalized to indicate the Holy Spirit. This means that the Holy Spirit has enabled John to see these things (see Revelation 1:10). *Coming down* is the exact same phrase as in verse 2; evidently, it is the same vision, but with additional detail.

> ▶ *(H)aving the glory of God. Her brilliance was like a very costly stone, as a stone of crystal-clear jasper. [Revelation 21:11].*

Glory is *doksa*, which means a "seeing, a notion, an opinion, an appearance." It comes from *dokeo*, meaning to think; it carries the idea of forming an opinion, an illumination; hence, the idea of a shining that often God uses to reveal Himself (see Exodus 33:18-22).

Brilliance is *phoster*, which means "light." **Like** introduces a figure of speech called a *simile* where John tries to describe what he saw. **Jasper** is *iaspis*, which is roughly equivalent to our diamond; hence, it was **crystal-clear**.

b. The New Jerusalem measures up to God's standards.

> ▶ *It had a great and high wall, with twelve gates, and at the gates twelve angels, and names were written on them, which are the names of the twelve tribes of the sons of Israel [Revelation 21:12].*

A great and high wall denotes a place of safety and protection, and a place where certain people cannot go (see Revelation 21:27). **Twelve angels** will be kind of an honor guard, because all the demons and Christ-rejectors will be in the Lake of Fire (Revelation 20:15). **Twelve gates ... twelve tribes** shows that Israel is represented, but so is the Church, with verse 14 telling of the "twelve foundation stones" – "the twelve apostles of the Lamb."

> ▶ *There were three gates on the east and three gates on the north and three gates on the south and three gates on the west [Revelation 21:13].*

Gates denote freedom and travel, Revelation 21:25. Ezekiel Chapter 48 gives names of the gates of Jerusalem during the Millennium: clock-wise from the northwest corner; Reuben, Judah, Levi, Joseph, Benjamin, Dan, Simeon, Issachar, Zebulon, Gad, Asher, and Napthali.

► *The one who spoke with me had a gold measuring rod to measure the city, and its gates and its wall [Revelation 21:15].*

Measuring is *metron*, which gives our word "meter." The **rod** (see Revelation 11:1) was about 10 feet long. The temple in Chapter 11 did *not* measure up; it was defiled by the antichrist. This New Jerusalem *does* measure up. This rod is **gold**, which denotes Deity, God's standard.

► *The city is laid out as a square, and its length is as great as its width; and he measured the city with the rod, fifteen hundred miles; its length and width and height are equal [Revelation 21:16].*

The city is **fifteen hundred miles** on a side, in the form of a cube or pyramid.

But you have come to Mount Zion and to *the city of the living God,* the heavenly Jerusalem, and to myriads of angels, to the general assembly and church of the firstborn who are enrolled in heaven, and to God, the Judge of all, and to the spirits of the righteous made perfect, and to Jesus, the mediator of a new covenant, and to the sprinkled blood, which speaks better than the blood of Abel [Hebrews 12:22-24].

► *And he measured its wall, seventy-two yards, according to human measurements, which are also angelic measurements [Revelation 21:17].*

The **wall** is 72 yards or 216 feet, according to human *and* angelic measurements. The number 72 is equally divisible by twelve; the number in Scripture for the nation Israel (see Revelation 7:1-8). The number 72 is also equally divisible by 24, the number in Scripture for the Church (see Revelation 4:4, pages 75-76). So, both Jews and Gentiles will live in the New Jerusalem.

c. The material of New Jerusalem is the finest quality.

> ▶ *The material of the wall was jasper; and the city was pure gold, like clear glass [Revelation 21:18].*

For **Jasper,** see verse 11. One can see through the wall! This is so the glory of God will not be hidden in any way. The **gold** is so **pure** that it, too, is transparent. We can tell from John's description that the New Jerusalem will be quite different from anything anyone has ever seen.

> ▶ *The foundation stones of the city wall were adorned with every kind of precious stone. The first foundation stone was jasper; the second, sapphire; the third, chalcedony; the fourth, emerald [Revelation 21:19].*

Sapphire is blue; **chalcedony** is blue with stripes; **emerald** is green.

> ▶ *(T)he fifth sardonyx; the sixth, sardius; the seventh, chrysolite; the eighth, beryl; the ninth, topaz; the tenth, chrysoprase; the eleventh, jacinth; the twelfth, amethyst [Revelation 21:20].*

Sardonyx is red and white; **sardius** is ruby; **chrysolite** is transparent golden; **beryl** is sea green; **topaz** is transparent yellow-green; **chrysoprase** is green; **jacinth** is violet; and **amethyst** is purple.

> ▶ *And the twelve gates were twelve pearls; each one of the gates was a single pearl. And the street of the city was pure gold, like transparent glass [Revelation 21:21].*

Pearls are white, which symbolizes purity (see verse 27). Notice that **the street** is singular, which means there is only *one* street in the whole city, or else it is generic for all the streets and gives its composition. If the city is a pyramid, then God's throne is at the top, and *one* street goes around and around all the way down. Perhaps the *one* street symbolizes the *one* way of salvation, Jesus Christ.

d. The glory of God illumines New Jerusalem.

> ▶ *I saw no temple in it, for the Lord God the Almighty and the Lamb are its temple [Revelation 21:22].*

I saw occurs here for the tenth time since Revelation 19:11. *Temple* is *naos*, which meant the Holy of Holies; that there is no such "temple" here shows that God is face to face with His people (Revelation 22:4), and there is total, immediate access to God. God Himself is the temple.

> ▶ *And the city has no need of the sun or of the moon to shine on it, for the glory of God has illumined it, and its lamp is the Lamb [Revelation 21:23].*

No need of the sun does not say that there *is* no sun; perhaps there is in the new heaven, verse l, but there is *no need for it*. *Glory* is defined by one theologian as "the sum of His infinite perfections." Another says, "it is the manifestation of His holiness." No sun or moon would show no need for seasons; thus, no need for time or calendars.

> He came as a witness, to testify about the *Light*, so that all might believe through him. He was not the *Light*, but he came to testify about the *Light*. There was the true *Light* which, coming into the world, enlightens every man [John 1:7-9].

> This is the judgment, that the *Light* has come into the world, and men loved the darkness rather than the *Light*, for their deeds were evil [John 3:19].

> Then Jesus spoke to them saying, "I am the *Light* of the world; he who follows Me will not walk in the darkness, but will have the *Light* of life" [John 8:12].

> So Jesus said to them, "For a little while longer the *Light* is among you. Walk while you have the *Light*, so that darkness will not overtake you; he who walks in the darkness does not know where he goes" [John 12:35 (See also 1 John 1:5-9)].

> ▶ *The nations will walk by its light, and the kings of the earth will bring their glory into it [Revelation 21:24].*

Nations is *ethnos*, which might be better translated as "Gentiles." *Kings of the earth* denote that the "nations" are still formed, but they are Gentiles. *Into* is *eis*, which means literally that; therefore, they are all saved people (see verse 27). All unbelievers have been purged from the earth.

> ▶ *In the daytime (for there will be no night there) its gates will never be closed; and they will bring the glory and the honor of the nations into it [Revelation 21:25,26].*

No night there shows we will never tire of serving God. *Its gates will never be closed* shows its perfect safety and security.

> ▶ *(A)nd nothing unclean, and no one who practices abomination and lying, shall ever come into it, but only those whose names are written in the Lamb's book of life [Revelation 21:27].*

Practices reveals the lifestyle of the Christ-rejectors.

> Now the deeds of the flesh are evident, which are: immorality, impurity, sensuality, idolatry, sorcery, enmities, strife, jealousy, outbursts of anger, disputes, dissensions, factions, envying, drunkenness, carousing, and things like these...[Galatians 5:19-21a].

See also Revelation 20:13-15.

For *Lamb's book of life*, see Revelation 20:15.

F. The River of Life, comforts and warnings, Revelation 22

1. The curse is lifted.

> ▶ *Then he showed me a river of the water of life, clear as crystal, coming from the throne of God and of the Lamb, in the middle of its street. On either side of the river was the tree of life, bearing twelve kinds of fruit,*

*yielding its fruit every month; and the leaves of the tree
were for the healing of the nations [Revelation 22:1,2].*

God (the Father) and God (the Son, the Lamb) are named, but the Holy
Spirit is symbolized by this river of the *water of life*. For further
symbolism see the water of life in John 4:1-26, the story of the woman
at the well.

For *coming from the throne of God*;

I kept looking until thrones were set up, and the
Ancient of Days took His seat; His vesture was like
white snow and the hair of His head like pure wool.
His throne was ablaze with flames, its wheels were a
burning fire. A river of fire was flowing and coming
out before Him; thousands upon thousands were
attending Him, and myriads upon myriads were
standing before Him; the court sat, and the books were
opened [Daniel 7:9, 10].

Street is still singular.

For *Tree of life;*

Then the LORD God said, "Behold, the man has
become like one of Us, knowing good and evil; and
now, he might stretch out his hand, and take also from
the *tree of life,* and eat, and live forever" – therefore
the LORD God sent him out from the garden of Eden, to
cultivate the ground from which he was taken. So He
drove the man out; and at the east of the Garden of
Eden He stationed the cherubim and the flaming sword
which turned every direction to guard the way to the
tree of life [Genesis 3:22-24].

Healing is *therapeia*, which gives our word "therapeutic." It is better
translated "health" in this context; probably symbolic of the
relationship of The Nations with God through the Holy Spirit (see
Jeremiah 31:31-34). Theologians call Jeremiah 31:31-34 "the New
Covenant." This prophecy was partially fulfilled for the Church on the

Day of Pentecost (Acts Chapter 2); it will be completely fulfilled for Israel at the Second Advent of Christ.

> ▶ *There will no longer be any curse; and the throne of God and of the Lamb will be in it, and His bond-servants will serve Him [Revelation 22:3].*

Curse is *katathema*, from *katatithami*, meaning to put or place down or away. We could translate "execration" from the Latin *ex*, "out of," and *sacer*, which means "sanctification;" hence, to be put out of sanctification or away from God's grace.

Bond-servants is *doulos*, which means a willing servant. Notice that even "sons" (Revelation 21:7), are still serving God. *Serve* is *latreuo*, meaning to worship by serving; it gives our word "liturgy," an order of service.

> ▶ *(T)hey will see His face, and His name will be on their foreheads [Revelation 22:4].*

They will see his face means Christ's unveiled glory.

> Then Moses said, "I pray You, show me Your glory!" And He said, "I Myself will make all My goodness pass before you, and will proclaim the name of the LORD before you; and I will be gracious to whom I will be gracious, and will show compassion on whom I will show compassion." But He said, "*You cannot see My face*, for no man can see Me and live!" Then the LORD said, "Behold, there is a place by Me, and you shall stand there on the rock; and it will come about, while My glory is passing by, that I will put you in the cleft of the rock and cover you with My hand until I have passed by. Then I will take My hand away and you shall see My back, but *My face shall not be seen*" [Exodus 33:18-22].

For *foreheads* see Revelation 2:17, 3:12, 7:3, and 14:1. These verses have special references to names. In Revelation 2:17, their special name is on an amulet worn around the neck; in Revelation 3:12, God's name will be written "upon them," the overcomers, the believers. In Revelation 7:3 God seals the 144,000 with His name on their foreheads; and Revelation 14:1 refers to this same 144,000.

> ▶ *And there will no longer be any night; and they will not have need of the light of a lamp nor the light of the sun, because the Lord God will illumine them; and they will reign forever and ever [Revelation 22:5].*

They will reign forever and ever – the same timeless period as Christ-rejectors will suffer in the Lake of Fire (Revelation 20:10).

2. John finishes with a comfort, a warning, and a benediction. Verses 6-21 make up John's appendix to the entire book. The prophecies end at Revelation 22:5, and he uses this passage of general exhortation to end the book.

a. John's comfort: Jesus' return *will not be late.*

> ▶ *And he said to me, "These words are faithful and true"; and the Lord, the God of the spirits of the prophets, sent His angel to show to His bond-servants the things which must soon take place [Revelation 22:6].*

These words are faithful and true, same as in Revelation 21:5. **Faithful** is *pistis*, which means committed, reliable. **True** is *alatheia*, which is intrinsically right; the same word is used for Jesus in John 14:6.

God of the spirits of the prophets means that God controls the minds of His spokesmen. The Greek, *prophatas*, equals *spokesman*, so that they preach, they proclaim, *His* message. **Angel** is *angelos*, which means messenger. **Bond-servants** is *doulos*, willing servants, the ones to whom God reveals Himself. God does not obligate Himself to manifest Himself to disobedient Christians (see John 14:21, quoted on page 229).

Shortly is *tachus*; it is the same root translated "quickly" in verses 7, 12, and 20. It means "quickly, speedily, shortly, or promptly." If the last translation, "promptly," is used, all time problems disappear. The verses can be interpreted as saying that when Jesus returns (which is the theme of the Book of the Revelation), He will return *promptly*. He will not be one minute late; He will come at the exact moment as predetermined by the Father.

Blessed is *makarios*, which means supernaturally blessed, or blessed by God. *Prophecy* is *prophateias*, a forth-telling; see Revelation 19:10. Prophecy is the testimony of, or to give testimony concerning, Jesus.

> ► *I, John, am the one who heard and saw these things. And when I heard and saw, I fell down to worship at the feet of the angel who showed me these things [Revelation 22:8].*

This verse describes the natural reaction of John to this divine messenger. Notice how honest John is in sharing his mistake with us. Christians should be this honest about their mistakes.

> ► *But he said to me, "Do not do that. I am a fellow servant of yours and of your brethren the prophets and of those who heed the words of this book. Worship God" [Revelation 22:9].*

Fellow servant is one Greek word, *sundoulos*, literally, "a willing servant with." The holy angels are fellow-servants with believers in Christ. Three groups are then suggested by the angel: (1) "of yours" [the Church], (2) "of your brethren the prophets" [the Old Testament saints], and (3) "of those who heed the words of this book" [the tribulation saints]. *Worship God* is imperative mood, the mood of command.

> ► *And he said to me, "Do not seal up the words of the prophecy of this book, for the time is near" [Revelation 22:10].*

Do not seal up is an aorist subjunctive of *sphragizo*, the same noun translated "seals" in Chapter 6. This subjunctive mood suggests that John was about to do just that, as God had commanded Daniel to seal up his prophecy in Daniel 8:26 to save it for the last days. However,

John *is in the last days,* the last dispensation before the return of Christ. The word translated *time* is *kairos,* which can be translated "season."

> ► *Let the one who does wrong, still do wrong; and the one who is filthy, still be filthy; and let the one who is righteous, still practice righteousness; and the one who is holy, still keep himself holy [Revelation 22:11].*

This strange verse is declaring what we have already seen in the Book of the Revelation: that behavior reveals condition of the heart, and that there is *no middle or neutral ground. Either a person is saved or not. Either a person has trusted Christ as personal savior or not.*

> ► *Behold, I am coming quickly, and My reward is with Me, to render to every man according to what he has done [Revelation 22:12].*

Reward is *misthos,* which can be translated "wages" or "payment" for services rendered. Every Christian will get their payment for their behavior at the *Bema Seat ...*

> For we must all appear before *the judgment seat of Christ,* so that each may be recompensed for his deeds in the body, according to what he has done, whether good or bad. Therefore, knowing the fear of the Lord, we persuade men, but we are made manifest to God; and I hope that we are made manifest in your consciences [2 Corinthians 5:10, 11].

... and every unbeliever will get their status in hell (Revelation 20:11-15). See also Matthew 11:20-24 where Jesus teaches degrees of punishment.

> ► *I am the Alpha and Omega, the first and the last, the beginning and the end [Revelation 22:13].*

This verse declares that Jesus Christ is eternal and sovereign.

> ▶ *Blessed are those who wash their robes, so that they may have the right to the tree of life, and may enter by the gates into the city [Revelation 22:14].*

Wash their robes is "do His commandments" in the King James Version. Both textual variances have good support, and both statements are true Scripturally. Titus 3:5 supports the first reading, and John 14:21 supports the second.

> He saved us, not on the basis of deeds which we have done in righteousness, but according to His mercy, by the *washing* of regeneration and renewing by the Holy Spirit [Titus 3:5].

> He who *has My commandments* and keeps them is the one who loves Me; and he who loves Me will be loved by My Father, and I will love him and will disclose Myself to him [John 14:21].

Wash their robes means washed by the blood of Christ by trusting Him as personal savior (see "without cost" in verse 17).

Enter by the gates into the city suggests that not all believers will actually live in the New Jerusalem. Compare Revelation 21:26, where "nations" is *ethnos* which could be translated "Gentiles," suggesting that the only "Gentile believers" living in the New Jerusalem will constitute *the Bride* (Revelation 21:9-10). The other believers will be the Gentiles saved during the Millennium.

> ▶ *Outside are the dogs and sorcerers and the immoral persons and the murderers and the idolaters, and everyone who practices lying [Revelation 22:15].*

Outside is the Lake of Fire. **Dogs** describes people of low morals. Notice the word "practices" again (see Revelation 21:27, which reveals an unregenerate heart).

> ▶ *I, Jesus, have sent My angel to testify to you these things for the churches. I am the root and the*

descendant of David, the bright morning star [Revelation 22:16].

The churches are finally here mentioned again, but we have not heard this word since Chapter 3, supporting the interpretation that *all the prophecies from Chapters 6-18 did not affect the Church because of the pre-tribulational Rapture.* **Root and the descendant of David** quotes Isaiah. 11:1 and **the bright morning star** fulfills Numbers 24:17 and quotes Revelation 2:28.

> ► *The Spirit and the bride say, "Come." And let the one who hears say, "Come." And let the one who is thirsty come; let the one who wishes take the water of life without cost [Revelation 22:17].*

Here is a three-fold invitation from Jesus, the Spirit, and from John, inviting anyone to come to God's grace for forgiveness.

b. John's warning: God's Word *will not be wrong.*

> ► *I testify to everyone who hears the words of the prophecy of this book: if anyone adds to them, God will add to him the plagues which are written in this book [Revelation 22:18].*

To everyone, not just the churches. **This book** could refer to the whole Bible, and in practicality it does.

> ► *(A)nd if anyone takes away from the words of the book of this prophecy, God will take away his part from the tree of life and from the holy city, which are written in this book [Revelation 22:19].*

This verse *does not teach* insecurity of the believer (see footnote 8, page 40), but is a warning to unbelievers that if they do not believe God's Word, there will be no hope for them. There is room for all people in heaven, but **rejection of Christ** will prevent a person from ever getting to the tree of life and into the holy city.

c. John's benediction: John's prayer *will not be silenced.*

▶ *He who testifies to these things says, "Yes, I am coming quickly." Amen. Come, Lord Jesus [Revelation 22:20].*

Yes is *nai*, a particle of affirmation; KJV "surely." **Come, Lord Jesus** is the only prayer in Scripture that is addressed directly to God the Son (excepting all the requests of the disciples directed to Jesus in the Gospel accounts). *Lord* denotes Deity and rule.

▶ *The grace of the Lord Jesus Christ be with all. Amen [Revelation 22:21].*

Grace is *charis*, God's unsought and unmerited favor toward those who deserve exactly the opposite. This prayer of John has been repeated over and over by Christians in every generation who will continue to do so until Jesus does come again.